T0340369

State and Society
in the Dominican Republic

Latin American Perspectives Series

Ronald H. Chilcote, Series Editor

†Available in hardcover and paperback

State and Society
in the
Dominican Republic

Emelio Betances

Foreword by Hobart A. Spalding

Routledge
Taylor & Francis Group
New York London

Latin American Perspectives Series, Number 15

The map on p. xvii is from Howard J. Wiarda and Michael J. Kryzanek, *The Dominican Republic: A Caribbean Crucible,* 2d ed. (Boulder: Westview Press, 1992), p. xxi. Reprinted by permission of Michael J. Kryzanek.

First published 1995 by Westview Press

Published 2018 by Routledge
711 Third Avenue, New York, NY 10017, USA
2 Park Square, Milton Park, Abingdon, Oxon OX14 4RN

Routledge is an imprint of the Taylor & Francis Group, an informa business

Copyright © 1995 Taylor & Francis

All rights reserved. No part of this book may be reprinted or reproduced or utilised in any form or by any electronic, mechanical, or other means, now known or hereafter invented, including photocopying and recording, or in any information storage or retrieval system, without permission in writing from the publishers.

Notice:
Product or corporate names may be trademarks or registered trademarks, and are used only for identification and explanation without intent to infringe.

Library of Congress Cataloging-in-Publication Data
Betances, Emelio.
   State and society in the Dominican Republic / Emelio Betances ;
foreword by Hobart A. Spalding.
      p.   cm. — (Latin American perspectives series ; no. 15)
   Includes bibliographical references and index.
   ISBN 0-8133-8681-0. — ISBN 0-8133-8682-9 (pbk.)
   1. Dominican Republic—Economic conditions.   2. Dominican
Republic—Politics and government.   I. Title.   II. Series.
HC153.5.B48   1995
338.97293—dc20   95-7669
                                                                      CIP

ISBN 13: 978-0-8133-8682-9 (pbk)

*In appreciation of my parents, José Manuel Betances and
María Altagracia Medina de Betances; and to my compañera,
Leticia Aldana de Betances, and my daughter,
Gabrielle Betances Aldana*

Contents

Foreword

Hobart A. Spalding

State and Society in the Dominican Republic represents a milestone in Dominican studies. In the pages that follow, Professor Emelio Betances of Gettysburg College seeks to explain the origins of the modern Dominican Republic by looking at social, political, and economic developments from independence in 1844 to the present. This effort, a particularly potent blend of theory and solid archival research, seeks to explain the formation of the Dominican state by looking at its nineteenth-century roots and to link that formation to processes that subsequently unfolded and that influence the current situation.

Betances's emphasis upon the late nineteenth and early twentieth centuries underscores his argument that the key events in the formation of the modern Dominican state preceded the first U.S. military occupation, which took place from 1916 to 1924. The study clearly links ongoing phenomena such as political instability, caudillismo, and dependency to a historical process that began shortly after independence and that deepened markedly with the growth of the sugar complex and foreign intervention after 1880. By the time of the U.S. intervention, socioeconomic formations already existed that conditioned the course of events and the ultimate outcome of the occupation.

The text makes a strong case for looking at Dominican development not just in terms of the intromission of outside forces but in terms of the dialectic between those forces and internal ones. Betances thus reasons that the ascension of Rafael Trujillo to power after 1930 should not be seen as an imposition by the United States or even as a "logical" or inevitable conclusion to the eight-year U.S. rule but rather as a result of the dynamics between imperial power and local economic, social, and political configurations. He concludes that internal factors rank alongside (if not over) external influences in determining final outcomes to particular historical processes. He reminds the reader that despite enormous discrepancies in the relative power between the United States and the Dominican Republic at all times, the former could not just impose its will upon the latter. This important point is often lost on those studying small states in the periphery.

Betances's arguments challenge much of the conventional wisdom of Dominican scholarship. He suggests, for example, that the dictatorship of Ulises Heureaux (1886–1899) and the regime of Ramón Cáceres (1906–1911) formed two distinct attempts to forge a modern national state. The fact that these attempts failed should not obscure the reality that they laid a groundwork and strengthened trends that the U.S. military government continued during 1916 to 1924. In reality, all three periods (those of Heureaux, Cáceres, and the U.S. intervention) make up the formative stage of the modern Dominican state. As such they provide, together, the historical and structural framework for the emergence of the thirty-year dictatorship of Rafael L. Trujillo (1930–1961).

As a historical sociological study, the book focuses upon the transformation of dominant class forces and their relationship to the origins and consolidation of the state. It further seeks to explain the impact of the modern dictatorial regimes—those of Trujillo and of Joaquín Balaguer (1966–1978)—on the process of state formation from 1978 to 1993. In doing so, Betances clearly links the Dominican past to the Republic's present. He argues, for example, that the regimes of Heureaux and Trujillo, as well as Balaguer's tenure in office, all illustrate how public resources have been used as a basis for the creation of economic (and therefore social and political) elites.

Solid scholarly work on the Republic has only very recently blossomed forth into a full-fledged international research field. Prior to the 1960s most people who studied the nation either did so for purely political reasons (i.e., to push their own particular point of view and often their own personal careers) or were traditional scholars who could afford the leisure of looking at the past. Only in the last dozen or so years has a whole new generation of younger researchers, many of them trained in Europe or the United States, systematically begun to investigate the important topics concerning the formation of Dominican society past and present. Betances belongs to this new group of scholars. His work thus complements that of people such as Frank Báez Evertsz or Roberto Cassá who have published on diverse themes, including social formations and the state, from both historical and contemporary perspectives. Betances also questions or seeks to modify positions put forward in the work of Ramonina Brea, José Oviedo, and Pedro Catrain, all of whom have written on aspects of state formation in the Dominican Republic.

In addition to being one of the most comprehensive studies about the development of Dominican state and society after 1880 and on the links between earlier social formations and the current situation, this study makes several other important contributions. It rests upon seldom-used sources, such as U.S. State Department records and materials in Dominican archives, most notably around the thorny issue of United States–Dominican relations, particularly in the late nineteenth and early twentieth centuries. The reader will find extensive notes and a substantial bibliography. This grounding in empirical data successfully complements the introductory material that discusses the theoretical literature on the state in general as well as relevant Dominican historiography.

This book, however, represents more than just a monograph by a leading younger scholar. In an important way, by examining the origins of the Dominican state and class formations, it follows an established tradition within Dominican letters represented, for example, by the writings of Juan Bosch (*Composición Social Dominicana*) or of Juan I. Jiménes-Grullón (*Sociología Política Dominicana*). The major difference between the work of these precursors and that of Betances lies in the fact that instead of sociological speculation or intuition (often insightful and, in many cases, subsequently found to be largely accurate), his work is rooted in specific theory and grounded by solid scholarly investigation.

As a study of the evolution of a weak and semicolonial state, this book has important implications not only for the Dominican Republic but also for the entire Caribbean. It raises important questions concerning the imposition of other strong men under seemingly similar situations, such as that in Nicaragua, where the Somoza dynasty immediately followed U.S. occupation. In the same vein, how does François "Papa Doc" Duvalier's reign connect with the U.S. occupation of Haiti, ended in 1934? Must the rise of Fulgencio Batista to power in Cuba during the 1930s be viewed purely as a creation of President Franklin Roosevelt's special envoy Sumner Welles and U.S. foreign policy? The study obviously calls for a serious reevaluation of the role of local and foreign forces in the historical process in the whole circum-Caribbean basin. It also suggests other questions. How did state formation in the area impact the emergence of local dominant elites in each case? And does a Caribbean typology of state and elite formation exist? Betances's work indicates that the answer may be yes.

This book, moreover, is not just an esoteric study of an abstract entity called "the state." The book successfully links past and present to make it one of the few historical interpretations of independent Santo Domingo. The last two chapters examine the era of Rafael Trujillo and the period since his assassination. They build upon the previous material to show how earlier formations strongly influenced later developments. Further, they look at the links between Trujillo and current strongman Dr. Joaquín Balaguer. As a historical sociologist, Professor Betances traces continuities in social formations, explicitly the persistence of clientelism and caudillism from their mid-nineteenth-century roots to present. At the same time, he skillfully analyzes the role of foreign influence, which has persistently impacted the course of Dominican history from the origins of the first Republic in 1844 right up to the present.

As an interpretive work covering the whole sweep of Dominican development, the book stands out as one of the few of its kind. It clearly makes a contribution to nineteenth- and twentieth-century Dominican studies. It also sheds light on the question of the development of the state in the Caribbean and Latin America.

Acknowledgments

In writing this book, I have become indebted to the many friends and colleagues who supported my efforts and encouraged me to see the work through to its conclusion. Cyrus Veeser read numerous versions of the manuscript with a critical eye and made insightful editorial comments. Barbara Metzger revised the final version and also made substantial editorial suggestions. From my student days at Rutgers University, I am indebted to Dale Johnson, my thesis adviser, Martin Oppenheimer, Mauricio Font, Samuel Baily, and Philip Stern. I thank those affiliated with Latin American Perspectives who read the manuscript, particularly Ronald Chilcote and Timothy Harding.

Conversations with academics in the Dominican Republic stimulated my intellectual curiosity; I thank in particular Juan Bosch, Franc Báez Evertsz, Roberto Cassá, Jaime de Jesús Domínguez, Miguel Ceara Hatton, Jaime Aristi Escuder, María de los Angeles Calzada, Margarita Cordero, Orlando Inoa, Frank Castillo, Wilfredo Lozano, Mu-Kien A. Sang, Diomares Caraballo, and Carmen Liranzo.

I am indebted to my colleagues at the Colegio de Historia in the Universidad Autónoma de Puebla in Puebla, Mexico, where I taught from 1982 to 1988. Particular thanks go to Sergio Tischler, Javier Mena, Marco Velasquez, Blanca del Razo, Facundo Arias, Miguel Angel Cuenya, and the late César Pellegrini. At the Universidad Nacional Autónoma de México, I would like to thank Pablo Maríñez, Carlos Vilas, Gerard Pierre-Charles, Susy Castor, and the late Agustín Cueva. Since moving to Gettysburg College in 1991, I have had stimulating conversations with Fred Kaijagi, visiting professor from Dar-es-Salaam University in Tanzania, and with Frank Chiteji, Lou Hammann, and George Fick.

I deeply appreciate the generosity of the Grant Advisory Commission of Gettysburg College, which allowed me to spend two summers in the Dominican Republic. I was therefore able to incorporate substantial Dominican documentation into this work and to speak directly with many persons involved in the political process. I should note here that all quotations from Spanish-language sources used in the text are my own translations, unless the citation comes from a secondary source written in English.

I am grateful to the staffs at the Gettysburg College Library, Rutgers University's library system, the City University of New York at Lehman College and Brooklyn College, the North American Congress on Latin America in New York, the New York Public Library, the Pontificia Universidad Católica Madre y Maestra in Santiago, the Universidad Autónoma de Santo Domingo, the Instituto Tecnológico de Santo Domingo, the Document Section of the United Nations Development Program in Santo Domingo, and the Archivo General de la Nación.

Last but not least I thank Leticia Aldana de Betances, my compañera, who read, criticized, and helped to prepare the final manuscript, and Gabrielle Betances, my daughter, whose time I took to write this book.

Emelio Betances

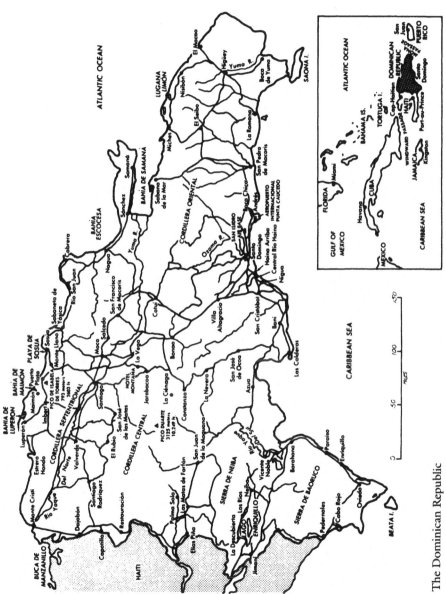

The Dominican Republic

Introduction: Historical and Theoretical Perspectives

Since the 1980s Latin America and the Caribbean have been undergoing a process of democratization. The military regimes installed during the 1960s and 1970s, having failed to fulfill their promises of economic and social prosperity, have been replaced by civilian ones. The models of development that the military employed excluded the vast majority of the population from political participation. It remains to be seen whether the newly elected civilian regimes will alter this situation. The extent to which democratization can be expected depends on the general patterns of state formation in the region.

Studies of these patterns are scarce, and most of them have focused on economic structures and general political development. This investigation complements earlier studies by focusing on the internal political process in the Dominican Republic in relation to constant foreign intervention. The Dominican Republic mirrors the larger reality of Latin America and the Caribbean in the sense that most of these nations at some point in their histories have had weak social and economic elites and a history of dictatorship. The rise of Rafael L. Trujillo in 1930 resembles that of Anastasio Somoza in Nicaragua in 1933. Nicaragua and the Dominican Republic were both fragmented societies; in both cases U.S. Marines intervened to set up national guards that eventually served as stepping stones for the dictators' assumption of national military and political control. Similarly, Haiti, Cuba, and Panama experienced repeated U.S. intrusions when their weak and fragmented societies were in crisis. Systematic study of the development of the state can therefore be useful in examining state formation and the structural obstacles confronted by the democratization process in general. If this study achieves its objective of explaining the tendencies of Dominican social and political development, it should contribute to an understanding of the complex issues of democracy and political instability in Latin America.

Historical studies on the state have been enriched by the works of Barrington Moore, Jr. (1966), Immanuel Wallerstein (1974), Charles Tilly (1975), and Perry Anderson (1975), among others. Arnaldo Cordoba (1977) has traced the origins of the Latin American states through the late colonial period. Anibal Quijano (1983) and Julio Cotler (1978) have produced insightful studies of the origins of the modern Peruvian state. Edelberto Torres-Rivas (1983) offers a methodological orientation for evaluation of the development of state apparatuses in the so-called less-developed nations. Oscar Oszlak (1981) describes the social determinants of state formation. In addition, the works of Marcello Carmagnani (1984), Alain Rouquié (1987), and David Collier (1979) are especially useful for developing a historical perspective on the origins of the Dominican state.

Traditional historiography has overemphasized the role of external factors in the development of Caribbean states, treating the Caribbean people as a "people without history" and ignoring the role of class struggle in the unfolding historical process. Although Bruce Calder (1984), Helen Ortíz (1975b), Paul Muto (1976), Mu-Kien A. Sang (1989), and others have provided excellent descriptions of the Dominican political process, they have failed to explain the character of the forces that have produced social change and the consolidation of political power.

Dominican historiography has traditionally relied on the caudillo paradigm to explain the development of political power. The caudillo paradigm has four salient features: (1) the repeated emergence of armed patron-client sets cemented by the personal ties of dominance and submission and by the common desire to obtain wealth by force of arms, (2) the lack of institutionalized means of succession to office, (3) the use of violence in political competition, and (4) the repeated failure of incumbent leaders to guarantee their tenure as chieftains (Wolf and Hansen, 1966:169). Julio Cross-Beras (1980) is a leading proponent of this paradigm, though one can also detect it in the more traditional work of Rufino Martínez (1985), Luis Mejía (1976), and Julio Campillo Pérez (1966). The paradigm has contributed to an analysis of the precapitalist character of the state in Third World societies, but it has overlooked the class character of the state in the transition from precapitalism to capitalism in these societies. I will suggest, in contrast, that nineteenth-century and early twentieth-century caudillo rivalries can be seen as a manifestation (though not a simple or linear one) of the class struggle in a developing society.

Class analysis has in fact figured prominently in attempts to explain the development of Dominican social structure, and here two main schools of thought have evolved. Juan Bosch, exemplifying one of them, claims that there was no Dominican bourgeoisie before the U.S. military government of 1916–1924 had established the material basis for its development (Bosch, 1982:214–226). Although no such class actually formed, he argues, it was upon this foundation that Trujillo was able to consolidate political power and become a functional substitute for it. In Bosch's view the only classes at the time were the petit bourgeoisie, subdivided into five strata (high, medium, low, lower poor, and very poor), and the landed oligarchy. The sugar plantations established during the latter one-third of the nineteenth century were "sugar islands" or enclaves. Their labor force was imported from Haiti and the Lesser Antilles and so did not constitute a Dominican working class. Thus, the political struggles of the time took place between the different strata of the petit bourgeoisie or between the petit bourgeoisie and the vestiges of a landed oligarchy (Bosch, 1984).

The second school holds that in the early twentieth century, merchants constituted a structurally heterogeneous bourgeoisie in that they received their profits in the form of surplus generated by capitalist and precapitalist relations of production. Franc Báez (1978), Roberto Cassá (1982b), Luis Gómez (1979), Carlos Vilas (1979), and Wilfredo Lozano (1976), for example, have argued that within this heterogeneous and complex social grouping the modern capitalist tendency was the most important determinant. Jacqueline Boin and José Serrulle Ramia (1981) and Juan Isidro Jiménes Grullón (1975) have gone beyond this in seeing the situation as a full-blown capitalist economy. None of these social scientists, however, has systematically analyzed the relationship between class and political power.

Ramonina Brea, building critically on the European debate on state theory (Hirsch, 1978; Holloway and Picciotto, 1979; Evers, 1979), adopts the perspective of Marx's notion of primitive accumulation, that is, "the historical process of divorcing the producer from the means of production" (Marx, 1, 1965:714). She argues that from this perspective the capitalist state can be seen as emerging from the contradiction between the violence of expropriation of the means of production and creation of the infrastructural preconditions for establishing a free exchange between capital and labor (Brea, 1983:29). The Dominican state was not, however, involved in the process of primitive accumulation until the U.S. military occupation of 1916–1924 (Brea, 1983:126). Again, although Brea's work contributes to an understanding of the location of the Dominican state within the emerging world capitalist structure, her concern with the derivation of the state from capital-labor relations diverts her attention from the role of class struggle.

Another interpretation of the origins of the Dominican capitalist state is provided by José Oviedo and Pedro Catrain (1981). They argue that although there were some elements of state formation prior to the U.S. intervention of 1916–1924, it was not until the intervention period that a state developed with sufficient material infrastructure to integrate the national territory, which was previously fragmented, heterogeneous, and without a principal economic regulator. Rosario Espinal (1987) has challenged this interpretation, suggesting that the U.S. intervention brought political and administrative centralization but not the project of a national state. In fact, she argues, the intervention worked against such a project: local elites had no notion either of the nation as a community of interests with a common destiny or of the state as a center of power for that nation (Espinal, 1987:47). This project would have to wait until Trujillo rose to power.

Oviedo and Catrain and Espinal see the Dominican nation and state as developing in accordance with the classical European pattern, in which the development of a market economy preceded the development of the nation as a community of interests based on a collective consciousness of a common destiny. In Europe the state itself became an instrument for shaping the development of nations (Tilly, 1975). The experience of Latin America was quite different; here the wars of independence helped spread national sentiments before the market had fully developed (Oszlak, 1981). Historians and sociologists have documented that the Dominican nation not only preceded the formation of the state but was closely tied to the development of the Haitian Revolution of 1791–1804 (Bosch, 1984; Cordero Michel, 1968; Cassá, 1986b; Pierre-Charles, 1974).

In contrast to Brea, Espinal, and Oviedo and Catrain, I will suggest that the outline of a capitalist state first emerged in the Dominican Republic with the Ulises Heureaux dictatorship (1886–1899). During this period the Dominican state began to express the interests of an emerging bourgeoisie dependent on sugar planters and merchants. By "bourgeoisie" I mean the dominant economic elites who own the means of production of the main sectors of the economy—industry, land, commerce, and banking—in short, the economic and political power of society. This political alliance foundered, however, because of the dependent integration of the Dominican economy into the international capitalist system and the collapse of Heureaux's dictatorship. Ramón Cáceres (1906–1911) continued the centralization of state political power that Heureaux had begun, but by the time he became president the U.S. government had full control of Dominican finances, and U.S. sugar corporations and banks dominated foreign sugar planters and merchants. Therefore, in helping to build the state he undermined the class that was necessary for it to be a national one. Rather than being simply the product of the U.S. intervention, then, the modern Dominican state experienced its nineteenth-century formative stages.

The emergence of the Trujillo dictatorship in 1930 and the transition to democratic rule from 1961 to 1993 were two epoch-making periods for the consolidation of the modern Dominican state. In analyzing the Trujillo period, I will build on the work of Franc Báez (1978), Juan Isidro Jiménes Grullón (1980), Roberto Cassá (1982b), Franklyn Franco (1992), Pablo Maríñez (1993), and Carlos Vilas (1976), who have been particularly concerned with the impact of U.S. interventionism on the process of state formation and with the role of the state in shaping social structure. On the transition to democratic rule, I will draw upon the investigations of Carlos Julio Báez and Otto Fernández (1975), Pedro Catrain (1982), José Oviedo (1983), Wilfredo Lozano (1985), and Roberto Cassá (1986), seeking to demonstrate that the regime of Joaquín Balaguer 1966–1978 was Bonapartist, that is to say, "above" the immediate interests of the local bourgeoisie, which was too weak to exercise social and political power. Aided by the United States, Balaguer imposed his political solutions on the country. In contrast to Heureaux and Trujillo, he used state power not to enrich himself but to create the general conditions for the development of a dependent industrial bourgeoisie. I will suggest that Balaguer's Bonapartist experiment ended in 1978 because the conditions that had brought him to power had ceased to exist: the bourgeoisie had consolidated its social and economic power. Finally, I will seek to show that in the course of the profound socioeconomic transformations of the 1980s, the Dominican state has been disempowered in the economic sphere, but the basic pattern of state formation has not changed. The Dominican state continues to be authoritarian and to obstruct the process of democratization.

In examining the formation of the state, I will draw a clear distinction between political regimes and the state. Following Fernando Henrique Cardoso (1979:38), I will define a political regime as the "formal rules that link the main political institutions (legislature to the executive, executive to the judiciary, and party system to them all), as well as the issues of the political nature of the ties between citizens and rulers." In contrast to a regime, the "notion of state refers to the basic alliance, the basic 'pact of domination,' and the norms which guarantee their dominance over the subordinate strata." In the words of Oscar Oszlak, "the state is a social relationship, a political medium through which a system of social domination is articulated" (1981:5). I will focus on the relationship between class and state, in particular on the way in which the state has shaped the dominant class forces even as it was forming and consolidating itself. The reader should be aware that this study focuses on class and state formation and not on the development of political regimes.

In contrast to the European debate on the capitalist state, which has examined the relationship between class and state in the imperial centers (Poulantzas, 1969, 1978; Draper, 1977; Maguire, 1978; Laclau, 1981, 1975; Johnson, 1982, 1985; Jessop, 1982; Gramsci, 1973; Hobsbawm, 1982), my research attempts to show how the international dimension of class relations interacts with local social structures in shaping the state in the periphery. State formation in the periphery occurs in the historical framework of an expanding capitalist system that needs local nation-states to organize export economies. Foreign capital and credit become components of local class structures and exercise direct political pressure on the state. When local political structures are unresponsive to the needs of capital accumulation on a world scale, imperialist powers attempt to restructure them. This has happened repeatedly in the Caribbean Basin, where capitalist states have tended to expand from initial structures largely imposed from outside through capital investments, financial control, and, finally, military intervention (Torres-Rivas, 1981; Quijano, 1983). Foreign intervention has played a crucial role in the development of the Dominican state. However, the internal political dynamic has also been critical to state formation because the state has provided the main source of revenue and social space for local political elites.

On the assumption that the concept of class struggle is anterior to the development of a full-blown bourgeoisie, I will propose the notion of an embryonic bourgeoisie, which through the experience of political oppression identified an opponent in the caudillos and sought political power in order to expand its economic base. In examining caudillos, instead of focusing on patron-client relationships and authoritarianism, I will explore the caudillos' relationships with wealthy merchants and landowners. In the nineteenth and early twentieth centuries there were two main types of caudillos in the Dominican Republic: ambitious military heroes of humble origin pursuing power, wealth, and prestige; and members of the elite seeking to preserve their political and economic interests. These caudillos established political alliances with merchants and landowners that conferred social significance on their rivalry and helped to shape the process of state formation prior to the U.S. military occupation of 1916–1924.

The U.S. military government broke the back of the caudillo political system by restructuring society and disarming most of the population. Regional caudillo rivalries were crippled by the new road network and the sheer firepower of the military. The policies of this government strengthened the state apparatus but did so at the expense of the social structures, creating the conditions for the emergence of a new type of national military caudillo who would use state power to forge a new elite.

The Trujillo dictatorship consolidated the modern Dominican state and initiated national control over the economy. In contrast to Juan Bosch (1984), who considers Trujillo to have been a functional substitute for the bourgeoisie, I will argue that Trujillo used state power to develop an elite of which he was the main but not the only agent. The Trujillist elite, linked to the dictator by family and business ties, controlled the main facets of the economy under Trujillo's hegemony. Trujillo promoted the development of capitalism on a national scale, but he failed to allow the development of a strong national bourgeoisie and state institutions that could survive his political regime. Again, as at the turn of the nineteenth century, the political incompetence of the local bourgeoisie prompted the United States to invade to rebuild the state within the framework of dependent capitalism.

From 1961 to 1993 the Dominican Republic experienced significant modernization. The economy was reordered on the basis of an agricultural-export model, and an incipient import-substitution industrial sector was established in the 1970s. The failure of this model resulted in a moderate opening of the political system and the end of Joaquín Balaguer's Bonapartist regime of 1966–1978. Concurrently, a new economic model based on free-trade zones, tourism, and banking began to develop. This change in economic models produced restructuring of the dominant social and economic elites without affecting the basic pattern of state formation. An authoritarian state, now removed from direct control of the economy, continued to inhibit the development of a democratic society.

1

Nineteenth-Century Regionalism, Political Struggle, and State Formation

The difficulties of state formation during the time period from independence in 1844 until the 1880s can only be understood in the framework of fragmentation of the Dominican economy and the social composition of the dominant blocs. The struggles between the emerging agrarian and commercial bourgeoisie of the Cibao region and the declining *hateros* (ranchers) and timber exporters of the eastern and southern regions, respectively, precluded the forging of a unified pact of social domination that could serve as the foundation for a national government.

The Rise and Fall of the *Hatos*

The agrarian structure of the Dominican Republic has historically varied from region to region. In the mid-nineteenth century three regional economic activities prevailed: cattle raising all over the country, tobacco cultivation in the northern Cibao, and timber export and small-scale sugar cultivation in the south. Throughout most of the colonial period and the first one-half of the nineteenth century, cattle raising was the nation's leading economic activity. When mining and sugar production almost disappeared at the beginning of the colonial period, cattle raising for export came to dominate the economy. During the seventeenth century cattle raising declined in the northern parts of the island and reconcentrated in the east, particularly after the Royal Ordinance of 1607 prohibited trade with foreign vessels. The western region became economically unviable, and most of the population moved south. In the course of the eighteenth century the prosperous French colony of Saint

Domingue (Haiti) gave a great boost to the cattle industry, becoming the main market for Dominican beef.

Antonio Sánchez Valverde, writing in *Idea del Valor de la Isla Española* in 1785, provides a good description of a *hato* (cattle ranch).

> The *hatos* ... are areas of largely dispersed and extensive fields that occupy many leagues for 400 to 500 head of cattle, or sometimes less, ... [*hatos* were] given on credit to slaves who hold the title of head shepherd and generally do not care about the master's profit; they are only concerned with earning enough money to buy their freedom. Even if one has two or three subordinates it is not easy to oversee the whole area because they are not sufficient to do all the work. (Sánchez Valverde, 1971:187–193)

On the average ten to fifteen people lived on the *hato*, slaves included, and social relationships were patriarchal. A relationship of trust between master and slave pointed to solidarity. Sánchez Valverde reports that masters used to have breakfast with the slaves before going to the fields to work with them at the same tasks; a social division of labor was all but nonexistent. In this type of setting slaves did not run away, as happened on plantations dependent on slave labor, but they rather saved money in order to buy their freedom.

Throughout the colonial period and even as late as the 1870s, the *hatero*, whose economic activity was concentrated in the east, was a key figure in Dominican society.

> On these vast segments of land with their corresponding natural boundaries, the ranch owner, prominent because of his economic position in the region, erected on what was called the seat of his *fundo* a manor house and other buildings where he lodged his family and servants ... corrals, presses for making sugar and molasses, as well as his *conucos* (small plots of land) for the cultivation of secondary crops, the ones necessary for the subsistence of his family and servants. On the ranch, the fundamental, necessary economic elements for the acquisition of domain over the occupied land were created. Those elements of cattle raising and agricultural crops created the material conditions on which the legal claim of a family's new patrimonial rights were based. (Alburquerque, 1961:17, quoted in Hoetink, 1982:2)

The *hatero* economy was vulnerable to the effects of events abroad. Relations between Spain and France were stormy during the French Revolution. A war broke out between them in 1793 that ended with a treaty signed in Basel in 1795 whereby Spain granted France the eastern portion of the island. Toussaint L'Ouverture was later to occupy it (in 1801) in the name of France. L'Ouverture, who had risen from slavery to become a French general, had fought for the abolition of slavery in Haiti, and slaveholders in the formerly Spanish part of the island were afraid that he would do likewise in the east. In anticipation of L'Ouverture's occupation, many landowners from the Santo

Domingo area emigrated to Puerto Rico, Cuba, Venezuela, and New Spain and took their slaves with them (Báez, 1986).

Bosch argues that between 1791 and 1805 rich urban families linked to the colonial bureaucracy abandoned the country, whereas most *hateros* remained to work on their lands. Despite the fact that the *hateros* were in economic decline, they nevertheless took up the challenge (with some help from the British) of returning the country to Spain in 1808. Spain was, however, unable to offer much economic support because it was in the midst of the Spanish-American wars of emancipation (1810–1824) and, at the beginning of this period, was itself occupied by France. Ironically, it took the *hateros* until 1821 to realize that no help from Spain would be forthcoming, and it was then that they declared the independence of the eastern portion of the island and renamed it Spanish Haiti. According to Bosch, "what is interesting about the *hateros* is that they attained political control of the country when they had lost economic power as such, since the market for beef had been lost and there was no other market to replace it" (Bosch, 1984:207).

The Haitian leaders who had won their own independence in 1804 took advantage of the weakness of the new government of Spanish Haiti to occupy it two months later. Haitian President Jean-Pierre Boyer feared that France would once more attempt to invade Haiti as it had done in 1814 and 1816, and his fears were strengthened by rumors that some French vessels had arrived in Martinique. In any case, the eastern portion of the island was the weak flank of independent Haiti, and Boyer occupied the east militarily in 1822, at the same time that he was attempting to persuade its inhabitants to join Haiti (Moya Pons, 1981:217). The occupation was generally welcomed. During the first few years of the occupation the Haitian authorities had some difficulties with the Catholic Church over land and the recognition of the archbishop of Santo Domingo. Although most of the church's lands were nationalized and some prominent families left the country after the failure of a revolt against the government in 1824, the occupation encountered no significant opposition until 1838. A proposed reform of the land-tenure system in 1824 was resisted by landowners because guaranteeing land to former slaves would strip them of their control over the labor force (Moya Pons, 1981:230–231). In the end the reform failed, however, and the *hateros* retained their social prestige and authority despite the end of slavery. Still, they could not reverse their economic decline in the absence of a market for beef. Because of their rejection of Boyer's agrarian reform, their domination of the peasantry, and the system of *terrenos comuneros* (communal lands) that had prevailed since the late seventeenth century, no class of smallholders emerged to take their place. The communal land system had its origins in "scarce population, low value of the land, the absence of officials qualified to survey the lands, and the difficulty of dividing up a ranch among the heirs in such a way that each would receive a share of the grasslands, forests, streams, palm groves, and small agricultural plots that, only when combined, made possible the exploitation of the ranch" (Hoetink, 1982:3). Because of the special requirements of ranching, lands were not divided when an owner died; instead it was customary to give each heir equal access to the fields for planting. This system produced independent farmers, but few of them were able to grow into large landowners, and the *hateros* continued to control large tracts of land (Cassá, 1979:168).

Tobacco Production in the Cibao Valley

At the beginning of the nineteenth century, tobacco emerged as an important crop in the northern Cibao Valley in response to European demand. In contrast to *hateros*, tobacco growers needed relatively small parcels of land, with small plots on the side for basic food crops. Tobacco was not demanding in terms of technique, capital, machinery, or infrastructure; a single family could raise a crop that paid for its basic needs. Tobacco cultivation soon became the dominant economic activity in the Cibao, where land was abundant. Until 1833 the level of production was about the same as when the eastern section was incorporated into Haiti, but from then until 1844 production increased 300 percent. In 1844 the country exported 1,380,000 kilograms of tobacco. That figure had more than doubled by 1851, and in 1860, 3,680,000 kilograms were exported. This figure dropped by one-half during the years of the War of Restoration against Spain, 1863–1865, but once the war had ended tobacco exports rebounded to 3,082,000 kilograms in 1867 and to 5,658,000 the next year (Cassá, 1981:19).

Commercial tobacco production and export engendered a new class structure in the Cibao region. Whereas producers made up an agrarian petit bourgeoisie, merchants constituted a full-blown, if diminutive, commercial bourgeoisie. The agrarian petit bourgeoisie received a boost from the Haitian-imposed abolition of slavery in 1822 as many former slaves became smallholders and had a freer hand in conducting economic operations. Plots devoted to tobacco production ranged from six to eight acres, and it was rare for large landholdings to be amassed. In the years before the second independence (1844), there was a significant increase in demand for tobacco in the international market, particularly in Bremen and Hamburg, and this brought an increase in the number of acres dedicated to tobacco production overall (Rodríguez, 1981:56–57; Báez, 1986:128; Rodríguez Demorizi, 1964).

Although tobacco is traditionally associated with small agrarian properties, petty producers were not always the owners of the land they tilled. Toward the end of the nineteenth century there were cases in which tobacco was produced through sharecropping or rental of land. In addition, small producers had to depend on intermediaries for the credit they needed to raise crops. *Corredores*, or brokers, exercised a great degree of control over these producers, and a social structure evolved whereby landowners and merchants extracted substantial profit from smallholders.

Despite the relative prosperity created by tobacco production and commerce, the level of development of productive forces remained low. The instruments of agricultural production included the Indian *coa* (a kind of hoe), the machete, and the spade. The plough, which might have facilitated planting, was still unknown. Furthermore, productive units remained dispersed in isolated towns (Gómez, 1979:36–38). Town and country remained relatively undifferentiated, and communication between towns was limited. Modern roads were nonexistent, and horses and horse-drawn carts were the only means of transportation.

Local and Foreign Merchants

Tobacco production generated considerable economic activity in the Cibao. Santiago, in the heart of the region, became the main market for the region's produce. Brokers from Santiago advanced money to producers before and during harvesting. Foreign merchants built warehouses in Puerto Plata, and throughout the nineteenth century tobacco was transported there on horseback from Santiago to be shipped to Europe. Poor transportation discouraged the importation of many products and disrupted the development of the internal market.

Two distinct sectors evolved in the development of the merchant class: foreign resident, and local. Foreign merchants attracted by timber and tobacco production began to establish themselves in Dominican ports at the beginning of the nineteenth century. By the time of the Haitian occupation, merchants from the United States, England, Italy, Germany, St. Thomas, Curaçao, Guadalupe, and Martinique were already established in Puerto Plata. "Around 1830 ... the Rothschild commercial houses of St. Thomas established a branch in Santo Domingo under the business name Rothschild and Cohen" (Hoetink, 1982:21), but it was not until the 1840s and 1850s that Sephardic Jews, almost without exception from Curaçao, became a notable part of the merchant community. Although foreign merchants exercised a great degree of control over local merchants, in the mid-nineteenth century a full-blown, if small, merchant class was developing in the Cibao. Most of its economic activity was directed toward retail commerce in the growing internal market. In this class one finds the brokers who advanced money that they received from large-scale merchants in Santiago or from foreign merchants in Puerto Plata; the funds went to producers throughout the Cibao.

Tobacco trade brought the development of an embryonic commercial bourgeoisie. Brokers established an effective network of credit whereby the growers became the peons of local and foreign merchants. The growers never accumulated enough capital to improve the quality of tobacco leaf and thus command higher prices. Ironically, they received no pressure from German merchants to deliver a higher-quality product. Dominican tobacco leaf was wrapped and sold as Cuban tobacco in cigars manufactured in Bremen and Hamburg. Writing in 1849, Victor La Place explained how the fraud was organized:

> Hamburg and Bremen, which receive most of the exports from Santo Domingo, order cedar wood from Havana to manufacture the boxes, the paper to wrap them inside the boxes, and the ribbons to fasten the cigar packages with the name of cigars from Havana. These cigars are made of regular tobacco and covered with a layer of tobacco from Santo Domingo. Thousands of these cigar boxes are often put into ships that return from the Antilles to give these cigars more credence. Later they are unloaded as cigars coming from Havana. (Boin and Ramia, 1979 Document No. 1:195)

This fraud allowed Dominican growers to cultivate tobacco in a non-capital-intensive and decentralized way while German merchants profited from the fraudulent sale of a lower-priced product.

Changing world market conditions, however, eventually made it impossible for Dominican tobacco to compete favorably in the German market. An oversupply of Brazilian and Dutch East Indian tobacco and the Franco-Prussian War brought a sharp reduction in tobacco exports (Ortíz, 1975b; Cassá, 1981; Rodríguez, 1981; Moya Pons, 1981). Michiel Baud notes that "the price of Dominican tobacco per quintal (one quintal is equal to forty-six kilograms) fell from between fourteen and twenty Dominican pesos in 1849 to nine pesos in 1872 and to four pesos in the 1880s" (Baud, 1987:136–138). Of course, the crisis faced by Dominican tobacco adversely affected merchants. Baud remarks that the number of local commercial houses in Santiago decreased from twenty-five in 1879 to six in 1884. Although some local merchants were able to shift to export of cacao and coffee, most had difficulty adapting.

While the development of a regional commercial class was being inhibited by local structural impediments and foreign competition, foreign merchants continued to dominate local economic affairs. During the first three-quarters of the nineteenth century, Dominican commercial navigation was restricted to the nearby islands, mainly Curaçao and St. Thomas, where European merchants had their representatives. These merchants advanced money and other commodities (clothing, machetes, spades, food) to tobacco and timber entrepreneurs to cover expenses between harvests and for the transport of products. A credit network developed that extended from Curaçao and St. Thomas to Dominican ports and finally to inland producers.

Although in Puerto Plata large-scale commerce was mostly in the hands of foreign merchants, in Santo Domingo local merchants had greater control over trade. On the basis of the archives of José Leandro García, Julio Rodríguez (1981:75) reports that in 1845 there were ten merchants in Puerto Plata: five Germans, three North Americans, one Frenchman, and one Englishman. In Santo Domingo, according to *Correspondencia Comercial de Santo Domingo* (1851–1877), of eighteen important commercial houses, ten were owned by Dominicans in 1851 (Boin and Ramia, 1979, Document No. 2:200–204). The document identifies four French, three Spanish, and one English house for the same year. Rothschild and Cohen were directly engaged in the commercial harvest of timber, and it has been estimated that they conducted operations that at times earned a total of 100,000 Spanish pesos annually, although business operation profits ranged on the average from 10,000 to 20,000 pesos.

Southern Landowners and Timber Production for Export

Beginning in the mid-1800s, a sizable class of landowners and timber exporters developed in the south. Large landholdings distinguished the south and east from the Cibao, where smallholdings were common. Citing documents from the national archives, Julio Rodríguez reports that in 1846, fourteen landowners who resided around the capital owned a total of 26,457 acres. One landowner had 885 acres, two had 360 acres each, another two had 180 acres each, and the rest had less than 135 acres each (Rodríguez, 1981:88). Harry Hoetink reports that large landholdings were concentrated in two areas, the eastern meadowlands and western Azua:

> In 1871 Don Domingo de la Rocha was considered the major latifundista in the country. He resided in the Capital, and it was believed that he owned a sixth of the extreme eastern section of the island in El Seybo province. Moreover, the family of the then President Báez was considered in that year as one of the richest property owners in the region of Azua. Outside these two districts, there are very few large landholders. Some had a thousand acres, and even ten thousand in a few cases. The rest is divided among small property owners. (Hoetink, 1982:4)

Timber had grown wild in the south since colonial times. Dominican timber was well known in France and England from the beginning of the nineteenth century on, and European demand prompted many *hateros* and merchants to enter the wood business. Woodcutting helped stimulate the country's economy, which had been in decline since the outbreak of the Haitian Revolution. As in the Cibao Valley, foreign merchants with some capital and stock entered into trade with the local population. In exchange for a strong foreign currency and badly needed commodities, a local woodcutter would agree to deliver a given amount of wood at the mouth of a river. Land transportation was limited by the absence of roads and the scarcity of porters (Domínguez, 1977a:58, 1977b; Boin and Ramia, 1979:68–74; Cassá, 1981:13–15). Timber production for export grew steadily throughout the

Haitian occupation. In 1822, 2,622 feet of lumber were exported. By 1830 this figure almost doubled, and after a minimal increase for the rest of the 1830s, 9,072 feet were exported in 1840; thereafter exports decreased to 6,009 in 1841, to 4,000 in 1842, and to 3,479 in 1855. Throughout the 1850s and 1860s there was a continuous decline in timber exports due to exhaustion of the forests (Cassá, 1981:16).

Southern landowners and merchants, however, continued to dominate national economic and political affairs. Landowners were often involved in timber exports; examples are Domingo de la Rocha, who financed Ramírez-de la Rocha, one of the eighteen largest commercial houses in Santo Domingo, and the family of Buenaventura Báez. Thus, the link between landowners and merchants was clearly defined. In contrast to the Cibao and Puerto Plata, where foreign merchants exercised a great degree of control over trade, in the south, local merchants controlled the ten largest commercial houses.

Sugar Production

Sugar had been grown for export in the country since 1515, but the development of a plantation economy was cut off by the Spanish prohibition of trade with the Netherlands, by the discovery of gold and silver mining in Mexico and Peru, and, most important, by the contradictions inherent in a plantation economy's dependence on slave labor (Cassá, 1979:83–91). During the seventeenth and eighteenth centuries, the country's economic structure shifted from plantations dependent on slave labor to primitive agriculture. Throughout the colonial period, sugar was produced primarily for internal consumption, and there was no significant quantitative or qualitative change during the Haitian occupation or the First Republic (1844–1861). In 1871 sugar was still being grown on a small scale in the south (in Baní, Azua, and the capital), where a few traditional plantations could be found. In Baní there were one hundred *trapiches* (presses) and around Azua perhaps one to two hundred in connection with some two hundred plantations (Hoetink, 1982:4; Báez, 1978:19). However, the level of technology of the sugar presses remained quite low, and the means of production in general was inefficient. Some presses were made of wood, others of iron, and they were usually powered by animals or waterwheels. The number of presses depended, of course, on the quantity of land held, and holdings tended to be small.

Political Struggles During the First Republic

The Haitian occupation had met with no serious objection from the dominant blocs in Dominican society for over twenty years, but from 1838 on the Trinitarios, a group of petit-bourgeois intellectuals, merchants, artisans, and others led by Juan Pablo Duarte, had been calling for independence. By 1843 the Trinitarios were notorious as nationalist militants and were taking full advantage of the reform movement in Haiti that had overthrown dictator Jean-Pierre Boyer. Duarte became the representative of reformists in the eastern portion of the island; he used the role to propagate his independentist ideas.

The Trinitarios fiercely opposed Boyer's economic policy, and the economic crisis that the country faced in the early 1840s contributed greatly to their efforts to muster support for independence. In the last years of his regime, Boyer forced Haiti's economic problems upon the inhabitants of the east by taxing merchants and, to make matters worse, he dramatically curtailed Dominican international trade by briefly closing Dominican ports (Rodríguez, 1981:168). Although the Trinitarios were interested in total political independence, to carry out their project they had to seek an alliance with *hateros*, timber exporters, and merchants whose aim was annexation to a foreign power. The declaration of independence on 27 February 1844 was rejected by Haiti, which made several unsuccessful attempts to invade the new republic between 1844 and 1855.

The first Dominican president, Pedro Santana (1844–1848), a *hatero* from the province of El Seybo and an annexationist, exiled the Trinitario leadership and had some of its major figures assassinated. Santana lost no time in contacting the United States, England, France, and Spain to offer them the country. Buenaventura Báez, a landowner and timber exporter, had plans for annexing the country to France even before independence was declared. As Dominican representative to the Haitian National Assembly, he had proposed this to Andrés Nicolas Lavasseur, French consul in Port-au-Prince; although the authorities at the Quai d'Orsay were not interested in establishing a protectorate over the Dominican Republic, local French agents had been busy promoting such a scheme (Tansil, 1938:124). Britain was not disposed to establish a protectorate over the Dominican Republic either but agreed to sign a joint declaration with France. The United States urged Haitian Emperor Soulouque to stop the hostilities against the Dominicans (Tansil, 1938:153).

Although the political leaders of the dominant blocs in the Dominican Republic were "nationalistic" in opposing Haiti, most were interested in pursuing their own personal interests rather than wanting to develop a locally controlled state. Personal rivalries over the spoils of office soon developed between Santana and Báez. Significantly, the one thing they had in common was their lifelong obsession with having the country annexed by a foreign power. Southerners had been hard hit by Haitian taxes in the late 1830s and early 1840s, and the near-exhaustion of the forests had brought a decline in timber exports. They saw annexing the country to a foreign power as a way of protecting their property and lives. In addition, many were of Spanish descent and disliked being ruled by black former slaves. Even when Emperor Soulouque fell in 1860 and a pacifist policy was implemented by his successor, President Fabre Geffrard, Báez and Santana continued searching for foreign powers to take over the country. Two factions emerged around their leadership, and throughout the 1850s, they separately opposed the leadership of the Cibao commercial bourgeoisie.

In an attempt to build a fortune for himself and his allies at the expense of the Cibao merchants, Báez increased the issue of paper money backed only by the good faith that merchants and producers placed in the government, and he distributed large sums to his agents to buy tobacco from Cibao growers for high prices. The devaluation of the currency led eventually to a revolt of the Cibao merchants, backed by the merchants of Curaçao and St. Thomas, and, with the help of Santana (returned from exile at their request), they battled Báez's goverment for over a year. From 1857 to 1858, the Cibao merchants allied with Santana were able defeat Báez, but this alliance could not be maintained for any length of time because Santana rejected the liberal Constitution of Moca, which curtailed the power of the executive. Santana overthrew the Cibao-supported government in July 1858 and proceeded to rule with dictatorial powers until the Spanish annexation in 1861.

Upon resuming the presidency in 1858–1861, Santana awaited the appropriate moment for annexation. An opportunity came with the U.S. Civil War and France's occupation of Mexico between 1861 and 1865. Santana sent his envoys to Spain, which was interested in regaining a presence in America and particularly in safeguarding its remaining colonies, Cuba and Puerto Rico. The United States could not do much to prevent the annexation of the country at the time, and the British, who sympathized with the South in the U.S. Civil War, did not oppose Spanish designs on the Dominican Republic.

Spain annexed the Dominican Republic in 1861, but the relationship proved difficult to maintain. The Spanish authorities subjected Dominicans to many new policies, devalued Dominican currency, and levied new taxes on both foreign and local merchants. A tax on horseback transportation, the only means of transportation for the majority of the population, was particularly unpopular. A large and costly bureaucracy came to rule in the name of Spain. The payroll of the Spanish public administration on the island was more than 3.5 million pesos when the government's income was less than 500,000 pesos. The new taxes levied on the Dominican population were expected to cover the difference, but this money was not readily available, and there were long delays in payment for government personnel. One hard-hit group was the Dominican soldiers who served as reservists in the Spanish army (Bosch, 1984:279–280). Moreover, many Spanish soldiers and bureaucrats had lived in Cuba, where they were used to dealing with black slaves, and they came to the Dominican Republic with prejudices. Finally, the Catholic Church attempted to regulate Dominican religious traditions. Under the pressure of these various factors, Dominicans of all classes rebelled against Spanish rule in 1863.

Spanish rule lasted only until 1865, but, ironically, it helped to define Dominican national values and thus strengthened a national identity. By the end of Spanish dominance, the power of the southern timber exporters and landowners had been eclipsed by that of the Cibao's tobacco growers and merchants. Santana died in 1864. Báez remained a powerful party figure, partly because many of Santana's followers had nowhere else to turn. In addition, a significant number of the Cibao's peasants thought of Baéz as their caudillo because he had created the illusion that he had helped them in 1857 when his allies bought their tobacco at artificially high prices.

Problems of State Formation

The Dominican state was formally organized as a liberal democracy in 1844. The first Dominican constitution, the Constitution of San Cristobal, established three independent powers—executive, legislative, and judiciary—and it provided for the creation of four ministries: Justice and Public Instruction, Interior and Police, Finance and Commerce, and War and Navy. The constitution directed the armed forces to be passive and obedient and established electoral processes for choosing the president and other government officers. It recognized the fundamental rights of the Dominican people and established a public treasury.

This constitution expressed the desires of a group of liberal nationalists who aspired to establish a political regime similar to those of the United States and Europe. It was, however, ill-suited to Dominican social conditions. Santana rejected the type of political regime proposed and argued that while the republic was at war with Haiti the president needed unlimited powers. Article 210 was amended, thus invalidating the constitution's liberal and democratic aspects (Rodríguez Demorizi, 1980:206). Tensions between groups competing for control of state power led to various subsequent revisions. In 1854 liberal forces were able to introduce a modification that consolidated civilian power, reduced military control, and even abolished Article 210. When Santana regained control, he abolished the 1854 reforms, once more ruling with dictatorial powers. Again, in 1858 and in 1865, Cibao-based nationalist political elites attempted to introduce major reforms to expand government institutions, but these efforts failed because the nationalists lacked the power base necessary to implement their constitutional projects. It was not until the Heureaux period (1886–1899) that viable bureaucracy was established and relative "national unity" was achieved. In the period between independence and Heureaux's dictatorship, no government was capable of undertaking any significant public works or expanding the state apparatus, and not a single modern road was built.

The difficulties in establishing national political institutions were associated with the country's economic regionalism and the consequent political fragmentation. Dominican social and economic structures remained largely undeveloped. No solid political institutions developed, and caudillos such as Santana and Báez took their place. These caudillos represented class-based interests that were threatened by the emerging power of the Cibao-based nationalists supported by a rising merchant class. The contradictory political designs of these political elites prevented the achievement of a pact of social domination that could organize political power.

Military Leadership and State Formation

Early on in its development, the military apparatus became the strongest branch of the evolving Dominican state. The military leadership of the caudillos obstructed the development of the liberal state and created an enduring legacy of authoritarianism. The wars the caudillos waged against Haiti (1844–1856) and Spain (1863–1865) contributed to a militaristic tendency within the Dominican state and civil society. Historically, the Dominican army had consisted of a small number of regular troops supplemented by volunteers in times of crisis. Santana organized these troops into an army that under his command acquired the characteristics of a national organization. The battles with Haiti forced the army to attain a reasonable degree of efficiency: "The regular army consisted of eight to ten thousand men. ... In a moment of unexpected invasion, the Government ... could immediately send one or two regiments to reinforce the borders of the South without leaving the capital unarmed" (Hoetink, 1982:95).

The army, strictly controlled by caudillos, should not be thought of as a modern regular army. Although it had officers and enlisted men, it was a political and military organization that basically responded to a single chief—Santana. When Haiti invaded in 1849, President Manuel Jiménes called upon Santana to use his prestige and authority to prevent the Haitians from crossing the border. Again, in 1858, when the Cibao merchants were fighting President Báez, they requested Santana's military assistance; everyone knew that hundreds and even thousands of peons and peasants would follow his lead. Nonetheless, these groups did seem to respond to a national military leadership, something that was not true after the Spanish annexation because during the War of Restoration the army was turned into a guerrilla force. It was not until Ulises Heureaux emerged as a national military and political leader that the army evolved into a "national" organization controlled from above.

Although Spain withdrew from the Dominican Republic in 1865, the prospects for the development of a social pact of domination had not changed. The essential difference now was that the leaders had a different social background. In the First Republic, the dominant political figures were either landowners or merchants, whereas after the War of Restoration leaders from the lower stratum of society were able to move upward through military service. Gregorio Luperón, the premier nationalist hero of the War of Restoration, was black and of humble origin. Another important nationalist and military leader was Ulises Heureaux, who had been Luperón's lieutenant and had also risen from humble beginnings.

The War of Restoration had created the possibility, or at least the illusion, of upward mobility for many army officers. Hoetink depicts the situation as follows:

> In 1865 a carpenter and a bricklayer who worked for Luperón ... could have the rank of colonel. ... In that same year there were already forty-five generals registered in the Ministry of War. ... According to Luperón during the seventies there were more than a thousand dispatches of appointment as general, issued principally by Presidents González and Guillermo. (Hoetink, 1982:96–97)

Roberto Cassá reports the commissioning of one hundred generals by 1865. By 1872 total state expenditure was 894,126 pesos, of which 647,938 pesos (72 percent) went to the War and Navy Department (Cassá, 1982a:22).

The increase in the number of officers on the government payroll added to the militaristic tendencies already present in Dominican society. The military, however, no longer had a hierarchical "organization" responsible to one man as it had during Santana's time. Hoetink suggests that a quiet restructuring of the army took place after the War of Restoration, whereby it acquired the characteristics of a marketplace breaking up into small groups that competed in offering their services in the political arena (Hoetink, 1982:96).

The marketplace character of the army was consistent with a patrimonial state in which the public and private spheres merged. Luperón used his own money to cover state expenses, but he also used the Puerto Plata customs house to enrich himself. In addition, he lent money to the state at 10 percent interest monthly, whereas European lenders charged 6 percent interest annually (Monclus, 1983:82). Heureaux was to make this personal lending common practice; in fact, it was impossible to distinguish his wealth from the state's. Foreign and local merchants were the financial reservoir for whichever caudillo led the nation. During the First Republic and after the withdrawal of Spain, whoever was in power borrowed from these merchants to fight the opposition while using the state's income to increase his own wealth. The struggles of the various political forces gave form to a state that no single class or group controlled. The alliances established between southeastern landowners and merchants in 1857 to thwart the aspirations to power of Cibao-based merchants illustrate the use of state power to promote the interests of particular groups. Similarly, under the veil of nationalism the Cibao merchants were seeking political power to provide themselves with an economic base. Thus, early on in its development, the state became a "terrain of struggles" over which the different factions of the embryonic dominant classes sought control.

Conclusion

The dominant blocs in Dominican politics were able to constitute a social pact of domination only in the latter one-third of the nineteenth century, when large-scale socioeconomic transformation had laid the foundation for a bourgeoisie based on sugar planters and merchants. A formal constitutional system had been established to provide for the transfer of power through elections, but no political group believed that its enemies would abide by such an arrangement. Constitutional changes occurred in times of political tension or when the opposition was strong enough to overthrow the government and enact reforms. Those in power were incapable of surviving a rebellion because they were too poorly financed to maintain a strong military force or to buy the alliance of potential political enemies. However, despite the numerous constitutional reforms enacted, the basic content of the Constitution of 1844 remained unchanged until 1908.

The dominant social and political tendencies of the period—annexationist and liberal nationalist—were to have a lasting effect on the political process of state formation. Liberal nationalism eventually emerged as the dominant political force. Many annexationists joined the liberals, who, once in power, became quite conservative themselves. As in most of Latin America, conservatives and liberals merged to exercise political power over the vast majority of the population. This new alliance promised the development of a strong national government that no longer sought to annex the country to a foreign power.

2

Capitalist Agriculture and Class-State Formation at the Turn of the Century

The Dominican Republic's social and economic structures experienced large-scale transformation in the latter one-third of the nineteenth century. Two agrarian systems evolved from these social changes: sizable capitalist sugar plantations in the southeastern regions of the country, and agricultural petty-commodity production for export in the northern Cibao Valley. The lack of integration between these two systems promoted the uneven development of Dominican society and constrained the organization of political power. The partial integration of the Dominican economy into the international capitalist system inhibited the development of these two sectors of Dominican society, and this was reflected in the weakness of the Dominican state.

Immigration and the Emergence of a Planter Class

A combination of world events facilitated the early development of a bourgeoisie in the Dominican Republic. These events included the Ten Years War in Cuba (1868–1878), which disrupted cane sugar production on that island; the Franco-Prussian War of 1870, which reduced sugar beet production in France and Germany; and the United States Civil War, which destroyed the sugar plantations of Louisiana. As in the rest of Latin America, local elites were interested in promoting immigration and offered concessions to immi-

Parts of this chapter appeared in "The Development of Capitalist Agriculture in the Dominican Republic, 1870–1924," *Middle Atlantic Council of Latin American Studies, Latin American Essays*, Vol. 6 (1993), pp. 23–39.

grants. The largest immigration was that attributed to the Cuban war, which caused more than one hundred thousand people to emigrate, nearly three thousand of them to the Dominican Republic. Although many of these immigrants were political dissidents who later left the Dominican Republic, a significant number remained. Some had technological knowledge and capital that they applied to sugar production and commerce. In fact, the Cuban capitalists, along with Italians, Germans, Puerto Ricans, and North Americans, constituted the nucleus of the Dominican sugar bourgeoisie. They joined the creole social structure by reinvesting their profits in the local economy and marrying into prominent local families.

Although sugar planters kept the citizenship of their countries of origin, they steadily began to adapt to the creole social structure. Juan Bautista Vicini came from Italy to start a sugar business in 1882 and went on to become one of the most successful capitalists in the country and one of the government's main creditors. He married into a Dominican family and joined the ruling circle of Dominican politics. One son, Juan Bautista Vicini Burgos, was president of the republic from 1922 to 1924. Alejandro Bass, a U.S. citizen, had worked as a machinist in the Cuban sugar industry, and in 1882 he had led a joint venture with F. Von Krosigh to develop the La Duquesa sugar mill. Subsequently he joined J. E. Hatton to establish the La Fe sugar mill. Bass obtained various concessions from the Heureaux dictatorship and apparently sought to establish a council of sugar producers with the objective of obtaining tariff-free export for sugar producers in 1888 (Sang, 1989:54). Unlike other sugar planters, Bass was keenly aware of his political and economic role in Dominican society. In 1902 he published a report entitled *Reciprocidad* in which he analyzed the international cane and beet sugar markets and asked the Dominican government to intervene to protect the Dominican sugar industry. One year earlier, his son William had acknowledged the need to pay property taxes to strengthen the Dominican state.

The Cambiaso brothers also participated actively in the economic and political life of the country. Originally from Italy, Juan Bautista Cambiaso took up residence in the country in the early 1840s and is credited with founding the Dominican navy. In the 1880s, the Sociedad Cambiaso Hermanos established several sugar mills, engaged in political activities during the Heureaux period, and received numerous government concessions. Like Vicini and Bass, the Cambiasos were creditors of the government during the Heureaux period and thereafter. The Lithgow brothers of Puerto Plata not only invested in sugar but also in a soup factory that enjoyed a twenty-year tax exemption. Federico Lithgow occupied various government posts and was minister of war between 1888 and 1892. The Lithgows also played a role as creditors of various Dominican governments.

Foreign sugar planters established an alliance with the Heureaux dictatorship beginning in 1886, and their sugar businesses prospered as beneficiaries of government loans and concessions. Their development into a Dominican bourgeoisie under the protection of the state was obstructed, however, by the partial integration of the Dominican economy and state into the world capitalist system.

The Development of the Dominican Sugar Industry

Between 1874 and 1916 the emergence of large-scale capitalist sugar plantations allowed the gradual formation of a class of sugar businessmen (Báez, 1978, 1986; Cassá, 1981; Gómez, 1979; Del Castillo and Cordero, 1982; Hoetink, 1982; Lozano, 1976). From 1916 to 1925, large conglomerates took over sugar production and commerce, drawing part of the Dominican economy into an international capitalist system controlled by U.S. corporations. The U.S. military occupation of this period helped consolidate foreign control of the Dominican sugar industry.

Although the first modern mill was founded in Puerto Plata by Charles Lyonaz, a Cuban, in 1870, the sugar business was to flourish in the south and east, which had extensive and low-priced meadowlands and a tradition of sugar production dating to colonial times. In 1874 the Cuban Joaquín Delgado founded the Esperanza, a successful modern mill near Santo Domingo. Juan Amechuzaurra, another Cuban, founded the Angelina two years later. By 1882 there were thirty-four cane plantations (Cassá, 1981:130).

In its early years the sugar business remained small-scale, based predominantly on individual ownership, but a tendency toward land concentration and capital centralization soon became apparent. In 1881, for example, the San Isidro Mill had 643 acres in cultivation and 568 to be cultivated—a clear indication of the prospects for growth. San Isidro also operated as a *central,* or milling center, receiving cane from thirteen tenants who worked 643 acres in all. In 1879, Porvenir had 540 cultivated acres, and, although records do not indicate what quantity was to be cultivated, an additional 180 acres belonged to the mill, possibly as pasture. Porvenir received cane from twenty-one tenants who worked a total of 360 acres (Cassá, 1981:130; Gómez, 1979:58–59; Báez, 1986:190; Sánchez, 1893).

Despite sustained growth, declining sugar prices in the world market during this initial period obstructed the healthy advance of a sugar bourgeoisie. The first acute decline came in 1881 as a result of overproduction arising from rapid expansion during several years of favorable prices and the availability of cheaper European beet sugar. Worldwide cane sugar production grew, for example, from 2,140,000 tons in 1876 to 3,538,000 tons just two years later. Moreover, in the latter year, production of all types of sugar reached 5,123,000 tons. In the crisis period between 1881 and 1889, thirteen of the important early mills failed. Most of these were in Azua, Samaná, Puerto Plata, and Santo Domingo and were sold for a fraction of their value. The

Ocoa Mill, valued at US$150,000, was sold for US$21,000. The Constancia, assessed at US$80,000, brought only US$7,000, and the Angelina, purchased only three years earlier for US$174,000, sold for US$30,000 (Ortíz, 1975a:348–352).

A second crisis developed in the mid-1890s, its most important cause being a record European beet sugar crop. In 1894, Europe produced some 6.6 million tons (1.9 million was German, 0.8 million French, 0.9 million Austro-Hungarian) in sharp contrast to the far smaller 3.4 million tons of the previous year. The dramatic rise caused a new glut in the market and a consequent drop in prices (Ortíz, 1975a:356). The world crisis did not, however, cause a decline of the new industry in the Dominican Republic. Despite the downturn for some mill owners, which provoked bankruptcies and closings, on the whole the crisis led to heightened competition and expansion on the part of foreign capital. Eleven mills shut down and about one dozen passed to new owners (Lozano, 1976:106), but in others low-level technology and individual capital gave way to more modern technology and centralized organization.

Sugar Planters and the State

The formation of a local sugar bourgeoisie based on foreign resident planters faced important trade barriers. Sugar producers had urged the Dominican government to negotiate a reciprocal treaty with the United States similar to the one enjoyed by Cuba, but no such treaty was achieved. Dominican sugar exports to the United States declined steadily, and by 1910 only 2 percent of Dominican sugar went to that market. In fact, Canada, at least temporarily, replaced the United States as the main importer of Dominican sugar. Dominican sugar had entered the Canadian market in small amounts until 1909, but in 1910 it amounted to one-sixth of Canada's sugar import. From 1913 to the late 1920s raw Dominican sugar constituted up to 20 percent of total Canadian sugar imports. However, Canada gradually began to rely on domestic beet sugar supplies, and by 1936 it imported no sugar from the Dominican Republic. During the 1930s, Great Britain gradually became the main destination for Dominican sugar (Muto, 1976:43–44). The greatest incentive to Dominican sugar producers, however, came with the U.S. Congress's passage of the Underwood Bill on 3 October 1913. This bill provided for a substantial reduction in the U.S. tariff to go into effect in 1914 and promised free entry by 1916 (Muto, 1976:43–44), but it was passed too late to help the foreign sugar planters, a significant number of whose mills had been shut down. Of course, many of the pioneers of the sugar industry were replaced by new corporate owners as property was concentrated in even fewer hands.

These economic changes had a ruinous effect on the local social class structure that the pioneers of the industry and foreign merchants had been forging. The Heureaux dictatorship, which expressed the political dimension of the emerging class structure, collapsed in 1899, and the state nearly went bankrupt. In the midst of this crisis, the United States began to play a bigger role in Dominican political affairs. A period of political instability ensued, and not until the years 1906–1911 could a faction led by Ramón Cáceres consolidate power. By this time, however, the emerging national bourgeoisie based on sugar planting and commerce had been elbowed out, and the U.S. government controlled Dominican finances. The Dominican state began to respond to U.S. political and economic pressure rather than to national interests. Under these new circumstances the state reintervened in the economy to create the general conditions for capital accumulation. By this time, however, most of the pioneers of the sugar industry were gone, and the agrarian laws of 1911 and 1912 that fostered modern private property and set up incentives for sugar production were meant for U.S. capital and the Vicini family's quasi-Dominican General Industrial Company.

The sugar companies were concerned about the obstacle to expansion presented by communal lands. Dominican peasants had been fighting eviction, and, unable to break the communal land-tenure system, the producers backed legislation that facilitated the appropriation of peasant lands. In an attempt to introduce modern private property relations into agricultural landholding, the government promulgated the Law of Agricultural Grants. In effect, this 1911 law called for the division of communal lands and the mandatory acquisition of legal titles. It did not specify that the lands had to be surveyed, however, and contained no sanctions against violators. As a result, an immense number of forged titles appeared as a means of expropriating peasant communal lands (Lozano, 1976:126, Moya Pons, 1986:541–544). In addition, the law allowed import and installation of industrial equipment at low or no duty, established tax exemptions, and removed duties on products for export for a period of eight years. It legalized foreign landownership and left unregulated the purchase of lands for the production of sugar and other export products. In 1912 a more comprehensive Law of Inscription of Rural Land Titles required that all rural land be registered within one year. Once again, forging of titles became big business and an effective way of dislodging peasants from their lands. Although these laws provided equal opportunities for national and foreign investors, it goes without saying that they benefited the sugar companies most. Traditional producers of crops other than sugar (cacao, coffee, and tobacco) did not need significant investments to raise and harvest their crops, nor did they have sufficient capital to introduce a technology that competed with sugar.

Although this initial state intervention in agriculture was not entirely successful, it was the action of a modern state helping to create the general conditions for capital accumulation. With the end of annexation in the late 1870s and the expansion of the sugar industry and commerce, the Dominican state acquired a degree of definition and determination, which helped it become self-sustaining. This process, of course, was rife with contradictions, because the state had emerged within an international economy that obstructed its development. When the state intervened in the economy it benefited foreign capital at the cost of undermining its national support base. Under these circumstances, neither the sugar pioneers nor the producers of other crops were able to take advantage of the new agrarian laws; they were marginalized from the most dynamic and capitalistic sectors of the economy. Thus, the prospects for the development of strong national government based on sugar planters and merchants collapsed. Foreign merchants were also pushed aside as the main beneficiaries of government loans. They were forced to turn to import commerce, whereas the creole merchants who generally occupied the lower echelons of the merchant class tended to join the traditional political elites in their fight to control the spoils of office.

The Consolidation of Foreign Corporations

The sugar firms achieved unprecedented control over land in a short time, but they did not change patterns of land use. Wilfredo Lozano has suggested that it was from 1917 to 1919 that the sugar latifundia were definitively established. The mills still held large areas of uncultivated lands, however, as was true during the formative period of the industry. In 1924, 114,128 acres were cultivated and 214,463 uncultivated; the amount of pasturing had increased to 76,507 acres. The dynamic potential of the sugar industry is reflected in the large amount of land not cultivated; this land was held in case of a sudden increase in world sugar demand (Lozano, 1976:157).

Extensive use of land from 1916 to 1921 produced unprecedented export levels. Until 1910 exports had not reached 92,908,120 kilograms, but after 1911 there was a steady increase to 122,642,514 kilograms in 1916 and to 183,610,637 kilograms in 1921. Volume, it should be noted, is not the only measure of the industry's success. The following year, with exports at 171,541,537 kilograms, the value had dropped to US$9,338,354, whereas in the previous year it had been US$14,338,354 (Muto, 1976:62). This fluctuation in sugar prices was principally due to the post–World War I economic depression. The effects of this depression on the Dominican economy were catastrophic. In 1920 a quintal of sugar had cost US$22.50, whereas in 1921 prices had dropped below US$2.00. Nonetheless, for a brief period the increase in world sugar prices brought some prosperity to the industry as well as a related, albeit moderate, multiplier effect in the southeastern region of the country. This period become known as *la danza de los millones* (the dance of the millions).

Falling prices after World War I had an extraordinary impact on the new sugar producers. Once again there was a concentration of mills in a decreasing number of hands. The Hatton brothers had inherited the San Isidro estate and had begun to expand its capacity through the purchase of machinery; when they became overly indebted, their property went to the Bartram brothers, butter dealers from New York. The Bartrams added the Consuelo estate, which the Bass family had overexpanded and encumbered with debts (Báez, 1978:37–38). In another takeover by a large monopoly, the Cuban Dominican Sugar Corporation absorbed the Barahona Company. The directors of the Barahona Company had thought that they could irrigate the lands around the town of Barahona in the southern part of the Dominican Republic. Surveys had made it clear that irrigation of these lands was an engineering impossibility, but even so H. J. Pulliam, secretary, treasurer, and a director of the Kelly firm of which the Barahona was a subsidiary, had gone ahead with the plans. The Barahona Company, like the Hatton Brothers and the Bass family, had run up large debts.

By 1925, foreign corporations controlled sugar production. The South Porto Rico Sugar Company, owner of Central Romana, and the Cuban Dominican, which built Central Barahona and acquired five other mills, were the largest corporations. These two owned eleven of the twenty-one mills grinding in 1925. Melvin Knight has indicated that

> a glance at the directorate of the South Porto Rico Sugar Company and the Cuban Dominican suggests that they are quite separate baronies in Sugardom. Mr. Schall, chairman of the South Porto Rico Board of Directors, is President of the American Colonial Bank in San Juan, Porto Rico. Mr. Dillingham, President of the South Porto Rico, is also of the above bank. Mr. Welty, another Director of the sugar concern, is a member of Mr. Schall's firm in New York, and Mr. Horace Havemeyer is also a director of both, besides being a member of Havemeyer & Elder, Inc., and thus a representative of the vague central organization of Sugardom. One director is on the boards of nine different electric power concerns. Two others sit at the director's table of various big insurance companies. (Knight, 1928:137)

A third and smaller group, the Vicini family, was the only remaining pioner sugar corporation. Others, such as Santa Fe, Porvenir, Boca Chica, and San Luis, eventually became affiliated with the Cuban-Dominican. Central Romana alone held 144,418 acres and had a value assessed at US$9,761,349.07 in 1925. In contrast, Italia, Azuano, and Ocoa combined were valued at only US$1,699,152.90 (Knight, 1928:139). In the Dominican Republic there was no longer room for individual capitalists; monopoly had taken over, and the most dynamic sector of the Dominican economy was incorporated into the international capitalist system.

The consolidation of the corporate sugar industry parallels the developments of the 1890s in that an economic crisis led not to a relapse but to expansion through restructuring of property ownership and land exploitation.

Even in times of crisis the sugar industry tended to expand. Lozano found that in 1925 investments in the industry had increased to US$20,331,830 even though no new land had been acquired. Investments had gone into higher levels of technology, making sugar a relatively capital-intensive industry. The apparently contradictory behavior of the sugar industry is explained by the fact that

> economic crisis in the sugar industry does not give rise to a low level of productive investment and low levels of production. It works in the opposite sense. This is due to the singular nature of the investments and to the high levels of capital necessary. Thus the owner of a mill increases productive investments in periods of crisis, hoping to get a better crop and thus compensating for the quantitative losses caused by a drop in prices. In the same manner, when prices are high production levels are increased, thus taking advantage of inflation. This represents a challenge to reach the equilibrium point in the market. In both cases we face a spiral from which escape is impossible unless productivity and price levels do not reach an equilibrium point. (Lozano, 1976:160–161)

Last but not least, the U.S. military government in the country helped incorporate part of the Dominican economy into the world capitalist system. In July 1920, it issued a Law of Land Registration as Executive Order No. 511. Bruce Calder has written that its goals were

> to "register without delay all lands located within the territory of the Dominican Republic" and to bring about "the demarcation, survey, and partition of the terrenos comuneros." To facilitate these matters, the law provided for a cadastral survey of the republic, a new system of land registration, and a new court, the *Tribunal de Tierras*, which would adjudicate cases involving land and administer the other aspects of the law. (1984:107)

The Land Registration Law served to legalize the false titles held by the sugar companies and to continue the expropriation that Dominican peasants had suffered since the 1890s. Nevertheless, its implementation faced two sorts of problems. The U.S. military government did not have enough money to implement a land survey, and, more important, it faced peasant resistance. Marlin Clausner has indicated that there was "resistance from small farmers who feared that the purpose of the survey was to take their land, but the attitudes of nearly all landowners was friendly" (Clausner, 1973:198). This difference in the attitudes of landowners and small farmers points to the class nature of the law. A guerrilla movement gradually evolved to resist the military occupation of the country, particularly in the east, where the sugar corporations often violently evicted peasants from their lands.

Timber latifundia controlled by U.S. investors rapidly evolved in this same period. According to Knight, on paper the lands dedicated to timber production in 1926 amounted to over three million acres. There were three important companies: Orne Mahogany, with approximately 500,000 acres;

Compañía Enriquillo, which claimed between 400,000 and 500,000 acres in the southwestern part of the republic; and the Habanero Lumber Company with vast holdings under quasi-legal titles in the province of Azua (Knight, 1928:151–152). Although the companies did not have effective possession of all the areas they claimed, they anticipated no serious problems in establishing title because the military government was more than willing to legalize their landholdings. The 1920 Dominican national census reported that timber companies held approximately 900,000 acres, and that cultivated and noncultivated timberlands combined amounted to 2,591,490 acres, with only 1,297,380 under cultivation.

Foreign control of the most dynamic and capitalistic sector of the Dominican economy had important implications for the development of a local class structure. The political loyalties and economic interests of the foreigners who had created the sugar industry differed from the interests of foreign corporate owners. The former had steadily become integrated into the creole social structure by joining prominent local families, reinvesting in the local economy, and participating in politics. The large foreign corporations that owned sugar business expatriated their profits to the United States and were not interested in becoming a part of the creole social structure. These new developments completely undermined the formation of a local bourgeoisie and the emergence of a national state.

The socioeconomic weakness of the local bourgeoisie provided the opportunity for continued U.S. intervention in the country. In 1916 the United States occupied the Dominican Republic militarily to set up a strong national government because it considered the local political elites incapable of self-rule. It has been argued that this occupation laid the foundation for the development of political and administrative institutions but frustrated the development of a sovereign nation-state (Brea, 1983; Oviedo and Catrain, 1981; Espinal, 1987). In fact, however, U.S. sugar corporations and bankers had already thwarted the development of a sovereign state before the occupation.

Modernization and State Intervention in the Economy

The Dominican state was not a full-fledged capitalist state at the turn of the century, but it had nonetheless begun to intervene in the economy to create the general conditions for capital accumulation. The dictatorship of Ulises Heureaux from 1886 to 1899 and the subsequent regime of Ramón Cáceres from 1906 to 1911 began to promote public works projects, and the U.S. military government continued them. Whereas Heureaux at least initially represented national political and economic interests, Cáceres did not. He continued to build the state, but he helped to eliminate the class that was necessary as the base for creation of a national class.

During the initial stages of development of the sugar industry, the horse was the basic means of transportation in the country. In 1884, the U.S. consul to Santo Domingo described the road system as follows: "There is not a single wagon road of any kind penetrating any more than three or four leagues into the interior. ... All of the inland traffic is carried on by means of animals. Goods are unpacked at the sea ports, placed in convenient packages, put upon the backs of animals and carried into the interior" (Consular Report No. 83, 1 August 1884). The industry's need for better transportation helped to end the isolation in which most of the Dominican population lived. As in most of Latin America, railroads were built essentially to serve the export economy. Rail lines were concentrated in areas controlled by the sugar industry, and when lines were established elsewhere the purpose was to connect a given region to a port rather than to build an internal network that would put an end to regional fragmentation.

Most of the early railroads were private lines built by and serving the sugar latifundia. In 1897, six plantations in the province of Santo Domingo had 110 kilometers of railroad lines. One plantation, the Santa Fe, had 30 kilometers of track and four locomotives to transport its sugar to the Ozama port. In San Pedro de Macorís, five plantations had 108 kilometers, and in Azua, three plantations had 72 kilometers. In the same year the Samaná Bay Fruit Company and the Compañía Frutera de La Romana, which raised bananas, also had a few rail lines and were building others (Hoetink, 1982:8). By 1925 the Department of Public Works reported 904 kilometers of track in the sugar region alone.

The influence of rail transportation was soon felt in other regions as well. Plans to build public railroads dated back to the 1860s, the first railroad being intended to join Santiago and the port of Samaná. The line was to cross the Cibao Valley through La Vega, a long-cherished objective of Cibao's producers and merchants, who needed rail lines connecting Santiago and Puerto Plata to facilitate transportation of their tobacco to European markets. In fact, in 1866 a concession had been given to Davis Hatch of the United States to build the connecting line. Throughout the 1860s and 1870s various concessions were granted, but none bore fruit.

The Samaná railroad was never completed, partly because of the difficulty of the terrain it was to cross, but rail lines were built from Sánchez to La Vega. The Central Railway was projected to connect Santo Domingo and Puerto Plata via Santiago, and during the Heureaux regime the Puerto Plata–Santiago leg was completed; a smaller section between Santiago and Moca was built later, completing only one-third of the intended route (Ortíz, 1975a:409–412). (See Map 2.1.)

Railroads introduced a new dynamism into the export economy and contributed to commercial activity. A dual movement evolved: products were sent to the ports from the interior, and manufactured products were shipped inland, where they were distributed to various commercial houses. Internal migration from various points in the Cibao region to the ports and main railroad terminals followed. Some of the migrants were merchants, lawyers, and doctors, but the great majority were workers who moved to participate in the construction of railroads (Báez, 1978).

Places that had been practically unknown before railroad construction suddenly emerged as important commercial centers. One of these was Sánchez, located on the northeastern coast. Once the rail linkages were completed, that port handled 9 percent of the value of Dominican exports and 11 percent of its imports; by 1892, 18 percent of all export value was being shipped through Sánchez. Even though San Pedro de Macorís rose meteorically in the same years, Sánchez maintained its relative importance. At the other end of the Sánchez railroad, La Vega also acquired prominence. Engineer H. Thomasset described La Vega in 1891:

> La Vega, though capital of the province of the same name, was nothing more than a large village in the center of the Cibao, equidistant some 140 kilometers from Puerto Plata and Santo Domingo and 100 kilometers from Samaná. These long distances and the bad state of the roads and consequent difficulties for travel during the rainy season had resulted in a forced isolation which naturally brought a languishing business sector and death to all industry. ... Today, thanks to the iron road, La Vega has its own life; it produces and ships its cacao and tobacco without fear of damage. (Ortíz, 1975a:411)

Towns in the south and east also grew significantly. For example, the capital city expanded from about 6,000 inhabitants in 1871 to 14,078 in 1893 and to 20,000 in 1898. Including nearby San Carlos and Villa Duarte would have brought the city's population to 44,000. San Pedro de Macorís, the center of the sugar industry, grew to 8,000 in 1898 and tripled in size by the 1920s. Higüey, a small village in the far east, grew from 500 people in 1800 to 6,235 in 1883 and to 10,000 in 1898. The 1920 Dominican national census reported a total population of 894,665. The province of Santo Domingo had 38,609 urban dwellers, constituting over 16 percent of the country's population. Santiago ranked second with an urban population of 20,495, or just over 2 percent of the total population. San Pedro de Macorís held third place; its urban dwellers reached 14,431, just under 2 percent of the country's population. Although significant, this urban growth must be kept in perspective: the rural population was still the overwhelming majority. The population of the province of Santo Domingo was 95 percent rural; Santiago and San Pedro de Macorís were over 97 percent rural. The rural population of the country was 745,771, or just over 83 percent (Lozano, 1976:214).

Along with the beginnings of urban growth, there was a limited degree of modernization. In the 1880s and 1890s telegraph and telephone facilities were installed in the main cities. Telegraph installations were inaugurated in

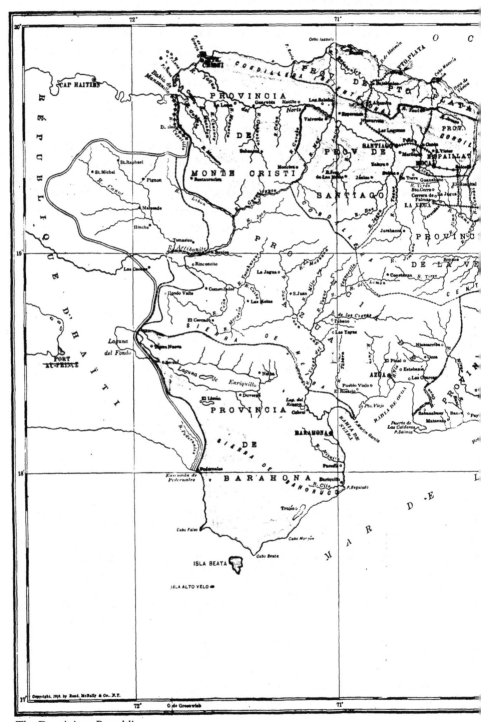

The Dominican Republic

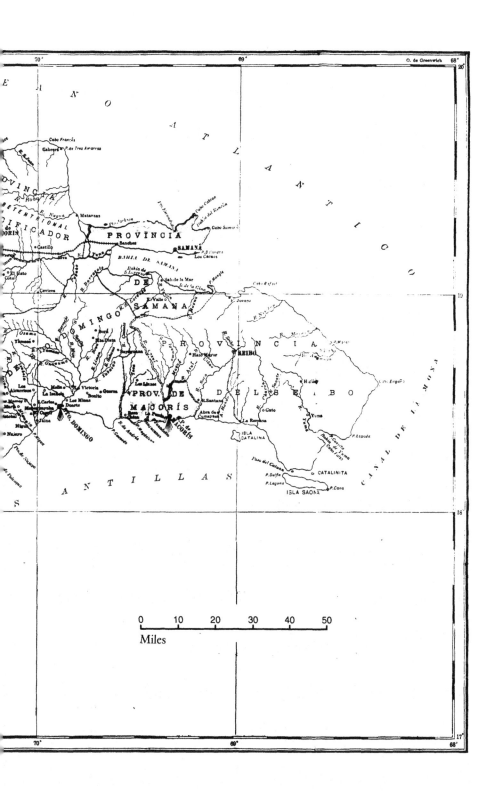

0   10   20   30   40   50

Miles

July 1885. By 1880 the country was finally joined to the outside world by cable via Curaçao and Venezuela. By the late 1890s the most important cities were connected by telegraph, and the nation's first telephone conversation took place in 1886. In the late 1890s private and public cars could be seen in Santo Domingo. The modernization introduced by the railroads and the new means of communication greatly diminished the isolation of interior regions and towns and allowed for the military and political control of the country that was essential for the development of the nation-state. Further, state-initiated railroads were the greatest single stimulus to the development of nonsugar export industries.

The Traditional Export Crops: Petty-Commodity Production

Whereas sugar and timber were mostly controlled by foreign corporate capital, traditional production for export remained in the hands of a local agrarian petit bourgeoisie, a class of small farmers unable to accumulate enough capital to invest in large-scale production. Dominican commercial agriculture for export throughout the nineteenth and early twentieth centuries was petty-commodity production. Until the 1870s tobacco had been the fastest-growing sector of the Dominican economy, but the rapid rise of sugar production displaced tobacco as the main crop for export and eliminated once and for all the possibility that the Cibao might emerge as the seat of national political domination. In fact, by the 1870s tobacco growers were grappling with both internal and external problems. First, as we have seen, the quality of Dominican tobacco had traditionally been poor (a cause of continuous complaint by German merchants), and an expensive credit system and general ignorance about tobacco culture by the Cibao's producers had inhibited efforts to improve quality. Second, local producers were dependent on the German market and were therefore susceptible to European price manipulation. Third, despite the construction of railroads that penetrated the center of the Cibao region, tobacco was still produced on small plots.

The political stability imposed by the Heureaux regime contributed to tobacco's prosperity in spite of the industry's problems. During the first three decades of the twentieth century, tobacco producers used railroads to export their crop but continued to depend on the German markets because their product faced a U.S. tariff and competition from superior Cuban produce. Thus, when the German market was blocked during World War I, Dominican producers faced disaster. Merchants sought to sell tobacco in the Spanish market, but a solution to their problem was found only when the United States agreed to purchase and transport the crop to Europe. In 1919 and 1920 the U.S. military government in Santo Domingo bought the tobacco crop, hoping to sell it when prices increased. (Because the measure had been facing effective political opposition since 1919, it may have been adopted to gain political support.) Tobacco prices did not increase as expected, however, and the government had to make up the loss.

Except for the years 1909 to 1911, tobacco exports remained flat, and by 1913 tobacco was third among Dominican exports. Cibao producers began to raise cacao in response to demand in the world market. Like tobacco, cacao was not a difficult crop in terms of technique and capital investment; mature trees would bear fruit for sixty to one hundred years (Pulliam, 1910:637–638).

Although cacao had been produced in the Dominican Republic for internal consumption, production for export did not begin until the 1880s. Export levels grew slowly throughout the 1880s, increasing from 111,320 kilograms in 1880 to 541,742 in 1889. This amount had almost doubled to 987,160 by 1892, and the following year saw a record crop of 1,911,116 kilograms exported (Gómez, 1979:63). Cacao producers benefited from good prices in the international market, improved transportation, and (in contrast to sugar) duty-free entry into the United States. Cacao exports not only increased steadily but compared favorably with sugar in terms of value in U.S. dollars. The revenues generated from raw sugar and cacao export were almost the same in terms of export value. In 1906 the country received US$2,262,912 for cacao exports and US$2,392,406 for sugar. Although it happened only once, it is worth noting that in 1908 cacao surpassed sugar in value, reaching US$4,269,047 to sugar's US$3,092,429. After 1913, however, sugar became the main crop by all criteria (Muto, 1976:62–63).

Despite sustained increase in cacao exports after 1910, internal structural impediments and international competition prevented a transition from petty-commodity production to large-scale capitalist production. Dominican farmers were unable to take advantage of favorable world cacao market prices to save and then to invest in order to expand and improve production technology. After 1910 the world cacao market changed and Dominican cacao had to compete with cheaper produce from Brazil and the African Gold Coast. Paul Muto attributes this to the fact that those with money to invest did not grow cacao: "Cacao growing remained the province of Dominican farmers who did not have access to large amounts of capital, and other Dominicans failed to invest in the crop. For the most part, cacao suffered no great decline; it simply ceased to expand. ... In the postwar period, expansion was negligible" (Muto, 1976:51). In addition, transportation was still a major limitation. Away from rail lines the roads consisted of mud trails, which made hauling costly. "To transport a quintal of cacao from the town of Yamasá down to Santo Domingo (100 kilometers) cost one dollar. The same quintal could then be sent from any port in the Dominican Republic to New York for 25 cents" (Bray, 1983:65–66). Thus, poor communication, monthly interest rates ranging from 2 to 6 percent, and international market competition created a bottleneck that partly explains why local cacao farmers were unable to transform themselves into an agrarian bourgeoisie. Otto Schoenrich, visiting the country during the U.S. military occupation, thought that cacao was a "crop for the poor" because the land and labor necessary were limited (Schoenrich, 1918).

Whereas tobacco and cacao were mainly Cibao crops, coffee was produced all over the country. Before the 1880s, it had been a traditional crop in Baní and San José de Ocoa in the southern region, and most producers shipped through the port of Santo Domingo. Favorable world market prices in the late 1880s led many of the Cibao's farmers to produce coffee, shipped through Puerto Plata. Later on, when the Sánchez rail lines were completed, coffee was also exported from the eastern Cibao. The Monte Cristi port also shared in coffee export. Insignificant through 1887, exports increased rapidly in the years 1888–1893 from 104,834 to 1,427,886 kilograms. By the mid-1890s an oversupply of coffee in the world market had brought prices down considerably, discouraging local producers (Ortíz, 1975a:383). Exports gradually increased until 1925. In 1906 production for export was 1,325,785 kilograms, whereas in 1925 it had not surpassed 2,666,313 kilograms. In the 1920s, however, coffee slightly surpassed tobacco, making it second to cacao among Dominican exports (Muto, 1976:65). It continued to be produced all over the country, though the Cibao continued to specialize in tobacco and cacao.

Coffee remained a product of small producers. José Del Castillo and Walter Cordero examined two contracts signed by producers and merchants between 1903 and 1907 in Baní, one of the main coffee-producing centers of the country, and found that all the plantations examined produced less than 2,300 kilograms. The average for all plantations was 920 kilograms. In Altamira, a list of coffee and cacao plantations for 1890 indicated that 73 percent of the plantations were less than 7 acres in size. In addition, the land was underused. In 1890, El Seybo had 799 coffee and cacao plantations with 1,794 acres of land, but these producers only cultivated 364 acres, 20 percent of the total acreage. A similar situation was found in Higüey. From a list of 531 coffee and cacao plantations that together held 967 acres, only 141, or 14 percent, were cultivated (Del Castillo and Cordero, 1982:100).

Thus the traditional export sector represented by tobacco, cacao, and coffee lacked the technology and the means of transportation to expand its production. Moreover, difficulties with credit and financing and a fragmented system of producing crops for export precluded expansion even when world prices were high. These obstacles amounted to structural impediments that prevented these industries' transition from petty-commodity production to large-scale capitalist agriculture and inhibited the formation of an agrarian bourgeoisie that could support the development of a modern capitalist state.

There is not enough information about the structure of large-scale landholdings dedicated to nonexport commercial agriculture of such crops as bananas, yucca, and other mixed crops in the northern Cibao to allow comparison with the leading export sectors. Even so, David Bray (1983:59–61) reports a 1903 "Honorable Mention" list of twenty-eight of the most "illustrious and progressive" farmers that provides some insight into the structure of landownership in this sector. Of the farmers mentioned, twenty-one were Dominican and seven were foreign, including two Belgians, two Italians, two Cubans; the United Fruit Company of the United States was also on the list. This distribution contrasts with that of the southern region, where foreign corporate concerns dominated the sugar industry. However, the fact that one-half of the landowners on the roll were primarily engaged in raising cattle and various other mixed crops points to their lack of development and thus to their inability to invest in production for export, which at the beginning of the twentieth century was the nation's principal avenue to wealth. Bray indicates that only four of those on the list showed any concern for technological innovation. Eight were involved in cacao production, but on the average their holdings did not exceed seventy hectares.

Hateros possessed much larger holdings, with some running to more than three thousand acres. Jacqueline Boin and José Serrulle Ramia (1981:50–55) report the existence of sizable *hatos* in the Cibao, near the city of Santo Domingo, and, of course, near the eastern sugar plantations, which used cattle to haul cane from the fields to the mills. However, the existence of scattered cattle ranches in the extensive Cibao region is not enough to make this group an embryonic agrarian bourgeoisie.

Conclusion

Examination of the development of the sugar industry and the main traditional agricultural export sectors at the beginning of the twentieth century reveals that the incorporation of the Dominican economy into the international capitalist system obstructed the development of a national bourgeoisie. It also shows that the denationalization of the leading export crop, sugar, suppressed the growth potential of a local bourgeoisie based on sugar production. In addition, the fluctuations of the world sugar market, trade barriers in the United States, and the continued indebtedness of sugar planters to North American creditors inhibited the growth of the local sugar industry.

Investments in the sugar industry initiated a transition to modern capitalist agriculture in the southeastern region of the country. The traditional export sectors, however, remained composed of an agrarian petit bourgeoisie. Despite the introduction of railroads into the heart of the Cibao, the small producers of tobacco, cacao, and coffee were unable to escape the structural impediments resulting from the fragmented system of export crops, insufficient credit, poor infrastructure, lack of technology, and serious international competition. However, unlike the sugar industry, traditional export agriculture re-

mained in the hands of local producers who lacked sufficient social and political strength to influence national political development decisively. Neither
the pioneers of the sugar industry nor the traditional export sectors could play
a leading role in the formation of the modern state. Marginalized from the
fastest growing sectors of the economy, local political elites perceived the state
as a way of acquiring a solid economic base. However, the continued U.S. intervention in Dominican political affairs blocked their access to government
largesse, forcing them into a subordinate role in relation to the process of the
formation of the modern state.

3

Merchants and the Integration of the State into the International Credit System

In the second half of the nineteenth century, a class of local and foreign merchants evolved in the Dominican Republic in association with political elites and the state. Like the sugar planters, these merchants were deprived of a main source of business and revenue; at best they could stake out the subordinate role in the import-export trade guaranteed them by the operation of tariff mechanisms. Their marginality in relation to the main economic activities of the country hampered their ability to influence national politics in the face of growing U.S. control of Dominican finances.

Immigration and the Formation of an Indigenous Merchant Class

Among the most prominent of these merchants were Spanish nationals, many of them immigrants from the postwar period between 1863 and 1865. At first they were disliked because of the war, but the prosperity they brought to the country gradually eliminated any hostility. In Santiago and Puerto Plata, Spanish merchants were famous for their business establishments. The Catalan Cosme Batlle was one of the richest and exercised a significant influence over the credit associations in most of the Cibao. José Armenteros of San Pedro de Macorís was a most prosperous merchant who led industrial ventures with local capitalists. Juan Parra Alba owned various companies involved in the manufacturing of rum, matches, chocolate, and ice, as well as a modern bakery in Santo Domingo (Del Castillo, 1981:197).

The immigrants came at a time when the creole social structure was undergoing changes due to the introduction of capitalist agriculture. The elites of the time were divided into the Sociedad de Primera and the Sociedad de Segunda. This division, established in the late colonial period, was very strict. Those with great prestige during the nineteenth century usually owned moderate-sized latifundia but had not amassed great fortunes. They were the remnants of a colonial society that had died with Santana and the failed Spanish annexation. Nationwide, there were about one hundred prominent families. Every town had its own circle of "patricians," as well as a group of frustrated aspirants whose education, race, culture, or relative wealth placed them above the masses (Bosch, 1959:32–39). By the last third of the nineteenth century many of these families had disappeared, but those ready to adapt to the new historical circumstances still struggled to preserve their social preeminence.

The agrarian transformation of the late nineteenth century brought with it the emergence of a new elite based on sugar planters and merchants. The assimilation of European, Cuban, and Puerto Rican immigrants into creole life and the generation of new wealth made admission into this new elite difficult. With the white newcomers, the issue of race became more important. As in most of Latin America, Dominican elites began to gather in social clubs, meeting places where members could discuss business. Agents of foreign capital frequented the clubs, where they recruited local lawyers to represent their firms. Many other matters, such as marriage and politics, were also discussed there (Carmagnani, 1984:124).

The most exclusive clubs were those in Santo Domingo, San Pedro de Macorís, and Santiago during the sugar boom. The Sociedad de Primera and the Sociedad de Segunda both had clubs. The Sociedad de Segunda included artisans, small merchants, storekeepers, teachers, and even unsuccessful lawyers, as well as white immigrants who had not been able to advance economically. Businessmen gathered in clubs that included members of the Santo Domingo Chamber of Commerce, Agriculture, and Industry. Since the elite was a small group, it was not difficult to meet at the Casa España with Puerto Rican banker Santiago Michelena, the director of the U.S. Banco Nacional, or with a member of the Vicini family. The small size of the national elite is further illustrated by the Dominican Republic's first national census in 1920, which listed fewer than 650 professionals.

Dominican elites strove to remain close-knit and exclusive, but the penetration of foreign corporate capital into the country robbed them of a solid economic basis for their distinction. They distinguished themselves from the Sociedad de Segunda and the masses but never developed an identity as a patriotic ruling elite. Even so, some of them, under the leadership of a group of nationalist intellectuals, opposed foreign investment and complained that the sugar planters had turned farmers into landless peasants. This faction was identified with Cibao traditional agricultural exporters of tobacco, coffee, and cacao and Cibao-based merchants who were probably excluded from Heureaux's distribution of concessions. At the same time, merchants, sugar planters, and members of the few old preeminent families capable of adapting to the new circumstances succeeded in forming a political alliance whose interests seemed to be expressed by the Heureaux dictatorship.

Merchants and the State

The Dominican executive exercised strict control over the institutions of government. The largest of these, the army, was controlled by the president, and it absorbed 60 percent of the government's budget. It used these resources not only to fight the wars against Haiti but also to fight the armed political opposition. Under these circumstances, no funds were available for public works projects or for consolidating government institutions. Customs collections represented over 90 percent of state income (Gómez, 1979:42, 69), which explains why the opposition always attempted to take over the customs houses.

Local and foreign merchants played a key role in these political struggles by lending money to rival caudillos. Between 1844 and 1869 Dominican governments were unable to obtain major loans from established European creditors, instead operating with money borrowed from individual European merchants established in Puerto Plata and Santo Domingo. Thus, merchants financed the government both indirectly, by paying the customs duties for imports and exports that formed the most important source of state income, and directly, with loans. In return for their loans, these merchants were granted exemptions from import and export duties (Hoetink, 1982:69).

In 1865 the government created a system of credit associations composed of local and foreign merchants who lent money to the government when it was in financial need. The government paid back the loans by allowing merchants to collect interest and amortization at the customs houses rather than exempting them from duties as before. Dominican political leaders sought to formalize the financial connections between the merchants and the state. Gregorio Luperón promoted the growth of these credit associations, further strengthening the association between the merchant class and the state. In 1881 the government agreed that Santo Domingo credit associations would provide for government expenses in Santo Domingo, Azua, and El Seybo as well. Similar arrangements were made to cover the expenses of Puerto Plata and Monte Cristi.

In 1884 the government exempted 50 percent of duties on products imported by Cosme Batlle. In 1893 it owed significant sums to Cosme Batlle and Juan Bautista Vicini (Sang, 1989:39–75). Bartolo Bancalari, an Italian resident in Samaná, participated in the credit associations of Samaná and had multiple business contracts with Heureaux's government. When Heureaux was facing political crisis in 1886, Bancalari lent him a substantial sum—and received numerous concessions. Still other important merchants having significant business relations with Heureaux were Juan Isidro Jiménes and Perello y Petit, both from Monte Cristi; the Ginebra brothers from Puerto Plata; Manuel María Castillo from San Francisco de Macorís; John Hardy, a U.S. citizen who resided in the Cibao; and Santiago Michelena, a Puerto Rican banker (Sang, 1989:61–75). Vicini in particular developed an intimate relationship with the Heureaux government. In a letter that reveals this association, Heureaux wrote:

> By reason of your having signed in my name the Contract that I copy in its entirety: Between the signatories Sr. Charles W. Wells, in the name of and in representation of the San Domingo Improvement Company of New York of which he is Vice-President, and Sr. J. B. Vicini as proxy of General Ulises Heureaux, owner of the credit that will be mentioned further on, the following has been agreed upon: First. The company commits itself to paying Sr. J. B. Vicini the sum of one hundred fifty thousand pesos in current silver in the following manner: from the month of May next the sum of two thousand ($2,000) monthly through the Caja de Recaudación at each month's end for two consecutive years, and at the end of the two years, the Company will pay the outstanding balance of the $150,000 in cash in current silver in a single payment. (Hoetink, 1982:74–75)

A sizable group of local and foreign merchants had developed around the credit associations and the import and export trade, and their very close association with the government gave the rivalry between caudillos and the emerging state a class character. The caudillo system was based on a patron-client relationship in which the "caudillo himself was the client of wealthy patrons who 'created and controlled' him as in investment for their own political and/or economic designs" (Haigh, 1964:481–490). The caudillos played an intermediary role between merchants and the state, dispensing government largesse to their faithful followers but also allowing the wealthy merchants who supported them financially to be rewarded at the custom houses with duty-free entry of their imports. These networks of political alliances forced a constant increase in public debt. Caudillos of humble origin rose to the upper echelons of society. Although classes in the strictest sense of the term did not yet exist, the class nature of the state became increasingly apparent as it acquired a certain degree of "national unity" and a viable bureaucracy began to be established.

Relations with European Creditors

The late-nineteenth-century initiation of a relationship with European banks constrained the development of a merchant class and undermined the sovereignty of the Dominican Republic. From the time of independence on, local and foreign merchants had benefited by charging high interest rates on government loans. Edward Hartmont and Company of London had agreed to lend £420,000 to the Báez Administration in 1869, and the contract required "all the resources of the State of Santo Domingo, its customs houses, rents and dominium" as its guarantee (Herrera, 1955, Document No. 2:241–245). In effect, this contract sought to establish a financial protectorate over the Dominican Republic. Hartmont and Company had made a first payment to the Dominican government in the amount of £38,095, but then it authorized Peter, Lawson and Son of London to issue a loan for the nominal £575,700. This alteration was not immediately communicated to the Dominican government, which then waited until 30 July 1870 to cancel the "unfortunate contract" (Herrera, 1955, Document No. 4:247). Perhaps Báez was too busy negotiating the annexation of the country by the United States and fighting the opposition led by Luperón; or he may have been unaware of the consequences of Hartmont's actions, which forced the country to pay for debts it had not incurred.

Political Instability and Indebtedness

The political instability that followed the War of Restoration brought increasing public debt. Customs revenue was often insufficient to cover the government's expenditure, and it was forced to borrow from local merchants to buy weapons and pay subsidies to its political supporters. The £38,095 that Báez received as part of the Hartmont loan went for bullets, guns, and supplies for the troops that were fighting Luperón's nationalist forces. Some of this money was also used for bribes and patronage jobs. Not a single pound sterling was used to build public works, a railroad, or a public building. Thus, the main cause of public debt was the continued insurrection, and that indebtedness meant that the Dominican government faced serious difficulties in obtaining loans from European bankers.

In 1885 the government of Alejandro Woos y Gil began to deal with a European committee of Santo Domingo's bondholders, but the Dominican representative, Eugenio Generoso de Marchena, was unable to negotiate an agreement. In June 1885 the minister of treasury and commerce reported that the government owed US$439,974 to local credit associations and US$189,246 to foreigners (Herrera, 1982:162). Most of the internal debt was incurred at an interest rate of 3 to 5 percent monthly, whereas European creditors offered loans at 6 percent annually. In 1886 the Heureaux government sent De Marchena to Europe again, this time with specific instructions to "recognize the £38,095 that the Dominican Treasury received from Hartmont plus interest at an annual rate of 12 percent" and "not to accept any negotiated transaction with the bondholders of the said debt unless the constitution of a bank or a loan was realized" (Herrera, 1955, Document No. 9:264–265). These instructions were obviously unacceptable to the Hartmont bondholders.

The process of integrating Dominican finances into the international credit system was a complex one. Local merchants charged very high interest rates, and although interest rates were lower abroad, the authorities were already encumbered by the Hartmont loan. Further, although Heureaux had defeated a Cibao-based rebellion headed by General Casimiro Nemecio de Moya, he had not completely consolidated his political power. A European loan would give the government relative autonomy from both the Cibao merchants and sugar planters and would help in dealing with an increasingly vigorous opposition forming around the figure of Luperón. In addition, paying off part of the internal debt would have a multiplier effect on the local economy and would induce merchants to support Heureaux.

Once more Heureaux sent De Marchena to negotiate a loan with the European creditors. Meanwhile, various foreign agents traveled to the Dominican Republic to offer suggestions for resolving the country's financial problems. In 1887 the U.S. consul to Santo Domingo, H.C.C. Astwood, offered to create a national bank. R. R. Boscowitz, a former Dominican treasury minister, signed a contract with Arthur P. Wilson of New York to provide a loan and to establish a national bank. Arrangements were also made with the Comptoir d'Escompte of Paris, and a deal had been reached when De Marchena completed his negotiations with Count Tadeo of Okzsa. Shortly after arranging for the loan, the count transferred his rights and obligations to Westendorp and Company of Holland, and De Marchena had to sign again with that company on 14 July 1888.

The Westendorp loan opened a new era in the process of subordinating Dominican finances to the international credit system. The loan, for a nominal £770,000, was intended to pay off all the internal debts of the republic and convert the foreign debt, borrowed in different currencies, into French francs. The Hartmont loan would be accepted at current London prices as "San Domingo 6 percent 1869 bonds." The Dominican government agreed to pay a yearly sum of £55,646 in accordance with an agreed-upon scheme of amortization. This amount represented 30 percent of the nation's annual revenue, derived almost entirely from customs duties. A general mortgage on all the income of the republic guaranteed the loan. Westendorp and Company would enjoy the supervision of the republic's customs houses, which meant a nearly total control of government finance. A customs receivership agency was to be administered by agents delegated by Westendorp and Company. In case any conflict arose, the contract provided for binding arbitration by the Dutch government. Cumulatively, these provisions amounted to a cession of the sovereignty of the Dominican state to a group of lenders supported by a European power (Herrera, 1955, Document No. 12:293-305). The opposition argued that it was unacceptable to place the country's main source of revenue under the control of a foreign company. Heureaux responded by publicizing Luperón's income, largely accumulated through usury, and by pointing out that the loan was to be used not only to pay off the Hartmont debt but also to cover the internal debt—a feature sure to please the merchant elite.

A large portion of the 1888 Westendorp loan did in fact go to service the Hartmont loan and retire a significant portion of the internal debt (US$800,000). After payments to local and foreign creditors were subtracted, the government received only a small portion. The money circulating as a result of the retirement of much of the internal debt did, however, turn local merchants into Heureaux's allies and help him significantly in the 1888 elections.

A second loan was arranged through Cornelio Juan Den Tex Bondt, a Westendorp agent who worked in the Puerto Plata customs house. Den Tex Bondt suggested a plan for a railroad from Puerto Plata to Santiago and, once Heureaux approved the proposal, he went to Europe to seek a loan for a nominal £900,000. The railroad project was submitted to Congress, which also approved it. In May 1890 the Heureaux administration signed a contract for the loan. Initially the cost of the railroad was estimated at £440,000, but £540,000 was spent on the first railway section alone. Considering that the loan was for £900,000 and that Heureaux had increased the amount dedicated to covering the internal debt from £108,000 to £140,260, the government used £37,977 to cover part of its expenses and the rest to cover interest and amortization of the foreign debt (De la Rosa, 1969:40; Herrera, 1982:197). Heureaux's increasing the amount devoted to paying the internal debt shows the influence of local and foreign merchants. For the first time, borrowed money was being used for a significant development project. At the same time, the building of the railroad was used as patronage or payoffs for political friends.

The government soon became dissatisfied with Westendorp's administration of the nation's customs houses. Den Tex Bondt proposed that the collection of funds from customs houses be centralized, allowing a reduction of interest and amortization payments to foreign and local creditors from 48 percent to 35 percent of import and export duties. Westendorp rejected these changes and informed the bondholders in Europe that the government had violated the 1888 and 1890 contracts by assuming too much control over customs. Following the crash of 1890, Westendorp and Company went bankrupt, but not before transferring its rights and obligations to a North American concern, the San Domingo Improvement Company (SDIC). The Dominican government had no alternative but to accept the change.

The government's problems were not limited to its dealings with Westendorp. In 1892 Heureaux initiated litigation against the French-based Banco Nacional de Santo Domingo for violating its contract. The bank lost, and in response the French consul requested the cooperation of Spain, Holland, and Italy in appealing the case to the Supreme Court. France, for its part, sent two warships. In the end, Heureaux managed to secure the support of the SDIC and the U.S. consul to Santo Domingo, who went so far as to furnish tools for opening the bank's security vault (De la Rosa, 1969:78–87; Sang, 1989:187–196). Finally, the Banco Nacional's owners had no alternative but to sell to the SDIC.

That France was unable to impose its will on Heureaux signaled a change in the relationship between the Dominican Republic and European lenders. The involvement of the U.S. consul in a dispute that other European nations had tried to resolve also pointed to significant changes in U.S.-Dominican relations. For twenty years, relations between the two countries had been distant. In 1870–1871 U.S. President Ulysses Grant had attempted without success to annex the Dominican Republic to the United States, but Dominican as well as U.S. opposition to the scheme led the U.S. Senate to vote against it (Welles, 1928:395; Rodríguez Demorizi, 1960, 1973). For some time afterward, U.S. influence over Dominican affairs diminished. Investments in sugar by U.S. citizens, however, and the SDIC's financial connections with Heureaux once again gave the United States an important role in Dominican political affairs.

For Mexico, Central America, and the Caribbean in general, the United States was gradually becoming a decisive political and economic force. In fact, the limited response of European creditors to U.S. intervention in their dealings with the Heureaux administration can be explained in these terms. Europe could not ignore the fact that the United States was now a world power with concrete regional interests. A few years after the dispute over Dominican finances, U.S. intervention in the third Cuban war of independence of 1894–1898 inaugurated a new period in U.S.–Latin American relations. The United States was now showing that it was able and willing to enforce the Monroe Doctrine.

Relations with U.S. Creditors

The new relationship with U.S. creditors set the stage for eventual U.S. control of Dominican finances and the incorporation of the Dominican state into the U.S. sphere of influence. The SDIC, registered in April 1892 in New Jersey, was managed by the New York law firm, Brown and Wells, which apparently enjoyed the backing of U.S. President Benjamin Harrison and Secretary of State James G. Blaine (Bosch, 1986:66). Armed with this unique mandate, the SDIC representatives traveled to the Dominican Republic to sign the necessary documents to make the transfer official. On 24 March 1893 Congress declared the SDIC the legal administrator of the customs houses of the country. The company was to pay the government 90,000 pesos in silver starting on 1 March 1893. The director-general of the customs receivership agency and the minister of the treasury were to appoint all officers in charge of all customs houses. The agency was to keep 35 percent of the money collected for the service of previous debt (Herrera, 1955, Document No. 17:337–343).

Once again a firm backed by a foreign power controlled the finances of the Dominican state and thereby undermined national sovereignty. Heureaux had succeeded in gaining a degree of autonomy from local and foreign merchants, whose economic and political interests were rooted in the Dominican society. He was now dealing with a U.S.-based corporation that had neither loyalty nor Dominican roots. This change had negative economic and political repercussions for the emerging bourgeoisie. Heureaux had expressed the planters' and merchants' political and economic interests, but with Dominican finances no longer under his control he was forced to distance himself from them.

The association of the SDIC with the Heureaux administration was replete with unscrupulous practices. For example, the law passed by Congress on 24 March 1993 was intended for public relations purposes only. The two parties had signed a secret contract on 28 January arranging a different distribution of payment of the internal debt. The public contract provided for a new issue of bonds in the amount of US$1,250,000 gold. These bonds or debentures were to cover the internal debt. The secret contract set up a different distribution that benefited local and foreign merchants: Cosme Batlle was to receive US$500,000 in Mexican currency; Jacobo de Lemos, US$102,689; Juan Bautista Vicini, US$152,706; and Eugenio Abreu and Company, US$11,490. If the Dominican government did not fulfill its obligations, the SDIC was not obliged to pay these debts (Herrera, 1955, Document No. 19:347–349). Although merchants continued to be important players in the political process, they were increasingly marginalized as U.S. concerns came to exercise control over Dominican customs houses and finances.

The SDIC covered Heureaux's private financial dealings, including his policy of lending money to the government at the highest possible rate. He in turn left the company free to do as it pleased in consolidating the internal and external debt, issuing bonds, handling money borrowed to build railroads, and so on.

The secret contract between Heureaux and the SDIC was just the beginning of government obligations to the U.S. company. The SDIC was also in charge of finishing the Puerto Plata–Santiago Railroad but failed to fulfill its obligation. For example, on 6 August 1897 the government was forced to issue a decree authorizing the issuance of US$500,000 in bonds called "Dominican Railroad 4 percent," to be delivered to the San Domingo Finance Company, a subsidiary of the SDIC (Herrera, 1955, Document No. 21:355–357). In addition, Heureaux entered into a contract with Den Tex Bondt, now an agent of the SDIC, whereby the government received US$225,500 in silver and agreed to pay 2 percent interest monthly. Again, the big loser was the Dominican government.

The Heureaux administration had seen various attempts to consolidate internal and external debts. Westendorp and Company had consolidated the Dominican debts in 1888 and reduced them considerably, to the benefit of the Dominican government. The SDIC had prepared a new debt consolidation when it began to administer the customs houses in 1893, and in the summer of 1897 it proposed still another consolidation that showed how thoroughly it controlled the Dominican state's income. On 9 August of that year Congress authorized the SDIC to consolidate the republic's internal and external debts with a US$4,236,750 bond issue. The income of the state was placed under the administration of the SDIC, and the 1893 gold bonds at 4 percent from two previous Westendorp consolidations were converted to bonds at 2-3/4 percent. This contract, like previous ones, provided for the arbitration of foreign powers—the United States, Holland, Belgium, Great Britain, and France—which were to have the final say in any conflict (Herrera, 1955, Document No. 23:360–366).

Although the debt consolidation by Westendorp had tended to decrease the public debt, the various consolidations of debt and issues of new loans carried out by the SDIC resulted in new debt. On 8 March 1900 the *Gaceta Oficial de Santo Domingo* reported that the foreign debt was US$21,111,528 in gold and that the internal debt was US$2,845,550 in gold and US$10,126,628 in silver (each silver dollar was worth one-half a gold dollar), a total of US$29,020,393 (Domínguez, 1992). The magnitude of these debts becomes clearer when we compare them with the national budget for those years. In 1897 the total income of the government was only 1,371,319 Spanish pesos. This amount had increased to 1,856,954 pesos in 1892 and to 4,794,509 pesos in 1894. In 1900, the national budget had declined to 2,242,685 pesos and dropped even more in the succeeding years (Domínguez, interview, 20 March 1992; Sang, 1989:287).

The public debt incurred during the Heureaux dictatorship was not used for corrupt purposes alone. During his thirteen years in office, Heureaux strengthened the Dominican armed forces. Supplied with three new warships and the newly built railroad, they now controlled most of the national territory, and this gave the state a degree of autonomy from the regional power brokers and allowed it to begin building a viable bureaucracy. In addition, it undertook various public works projects, including telegraphic communications, bridges, port facilities, and a railroad between Sánchez and La Vega and between Santiago and Puerto Plata. However, Heureaux's relations with the SDIC and his implementation of inappropriate economic policies eventually forced his government into a fatal political crisis. The public debt made it impossible for him to allocate large subsidies (patronage jobs and bribery of opponents) to his political machine, and he kept himself in power through secret loans from the SDIC, sugar planters, and local merchants. When he could no longer raise money he began to issue paper money supposedly backed by the

Banco Nacional de Santo Domingo, an SDIC ally. On 23 January 1899 Heureaux had issued 2,600,000 pesos in bills in addition to the 3,600,000 pesos issued in March 1898 (Bosch, 1986:202). These "papeletas de Lilís" were rejected by merchants for lacking any real backing, and in 1899 a general strike was called in protest. Heureaux attempted to resolve the ensuing economic and political crisis by publicly burning large quantities of inflated bills in Sánchez and in La Vega, but when he reached Moca on 26 July 1899 he was assassinated.

The two leading political figures of the time were Horacio Vásquez and Juan Isidro Jiménes. Jiménes, a Monte Cristi merchant and landowner, had become a national political hero after an unsuccessful expedition to overthrow Heureaux in 1898. Vásquez, a Moca landowner, had become active in the ongoing movement to eliminate Heureaux thereafter, and after the assassination he had asked Jiménes to return from exile to take power. However, these two leaders soon parted company over the handling of Heureaux's debts to the SDIC. There were no substantial political differences between the leading political forces in the country, nor did they represent different social classes. In any case, whoever led the nation possessed at best a qualified sovereignty. The United States negotiated with the Dominican governments as one leader succeeded another. When Vásquez overthrew Jiménes in April 1902, he proceeded to negotiate with John T. Abbott, the U.S. commercial agent in Santo Domingo. Abbott was also vice president of the SDIC, and his dual role indicated how far the United States was willing to go to support that company. Vásquez and his followers, who during the Jiménes administration had opposed any negotiation with the SDIC or acceptance of foreign arbitration, agreed to sign a protocol in 1903 according to which they recognized a debt of US$4,500,000 in gold to the SDIC and its subsidiaries. This agreement, like the previous ones, provided for the creation of a tribunal of arbitration, composed of three members: the first designated by the president of United States, the second named by the Dominican government, and the third selected jointly. If no agreement emerged, the Supreme Court of the United States was to designate the third member (Herrera, 1955, Document No. 31:404–7).

The overthrow of Vásquez in March 1903 did not halt these negotiations. Alejandro Woos y Gil, formerly vice president under Heureaux, replaced Vásquez, and he himself was replaced, in accordance with a brief agreement between Vásquez and Jiménes, by Carlos Morales Languasco. Morales Languasco remained in power long enough to sign an arbitration award on 14 July 1904 whereby the SDIC affair was resolved. The Dominican Republic was ordered to pay the SDIC US$4,500,000 in monthly payments of US$37,500 each over the first two years and US$41,666 after the third year, with an annual interest rate of 4 percent (Rippy, 1937:419–457).

Although the alliance that brought Morales Languasco to power disintegrated quickly, he signed an interim agreement on 7 February 1905 whereby the United States was to take charge of Dominican customs delivery. Forty-five percent of the customs collections would go to the Dominican government and 55 percent was to pay for the amortization and interest on the republic's debts and the cost of the customs receivership administration (Message from the President of the United States, 1905:343). By year's end, however, he had lost all his support and his vice president, Ramón Cáceres (a protégé of Horacio Vásquez), had gained the favor of the cabinet. In this difficult situation, having failed in an attempt to dissolve his cabinet, he resigned. In January 1906 Cáceres took full control of the government and replaced the president.

The struggles over state power that followed Heureaux's downfall show that politics had become a principal mechanism for amassing wealth. The political institutions that Heureaux had sought to develop were collapsing. The army resumed the character of a marketplace, and the state once again became a battlefield for regional political forces. These forces represented the remnants of an emerging national bourgeoisie disabled by foreign corporate investment and credit. Robbed of an economic base, fragmented local elites sought to control the state and thus acquire access to the revenues of the customs houses. However, it was no longer possible for them to control state power, because from 1904 on the United States was managing Dominican finances.

The Convention of 1907

American involvement in Dominican affairs increased after the signing of the interim agreement. Aware of European debt claims against the republic and the danger of foreign meddling in Dominican affairs, in April 1905 Theodore Roosevelt sent Jacob Hollander as his special representative to the Dominican Republic to look into his southern neighbor's debts. Hollander prepared a confidential report, *The Debt of Santo Domingo*, that Roosevelt used in developing his policy toward the Dominican Republic. Hollander classified outstanding debts as follows:

(1) the bonded debt, comprising public indebtedness represented by outstanding bonds that amounted to $17,670,312; (2) the liquidated debt, consisting of items secured by international protocols or by formal contracts coming to $9,595,530; (3) floating debt, consisting of admitted indebtedness, neither funded nor secured, but evidenced by public obligations in the amount of $1,553,507; (4) declared claims, presented for foreign reimbursement or indemnity but not expressly recognized by the government, totalling $7,450,053; and (5) undeclared claims of the same kind as in the previous category but not yet for-

mally presented for payment. In total, the debt amounted to $40,269,404. (U.S. Senate, 1905:16–32; Hollander quoted by Schoenrich, 1918:353)

In 1900, as we have seen, the government's internal and external debts had reportedly amounted to US$29,020,393. This substantial difference was always a source of conflict between Dominican authorities and foreign creditors, and Hollander himself was quite aware of this. Speaking to the United States Senate Committee on Foreign Relations on 16 January 1907, he said:

> I do not think any of them are valid debts, in the sense that public debts in the United States are, but such as they are, something must be done with them. ... There is little that is credible in the financial past of Santo Domingo. But granting this, we are now confronted by recognized claims, and we can not go back to the beginning of things. These debts have been created, have been acknowledged by the Republic, and have been in large part secured by an assignment of custom houses to foreign government. (U.S. Senate, 1907:1, 17)

Hollander's acknowledgment that the Dominican debts were invalid supports the interpretation that European and U.S. creditors had made substantial profits from their financial dealings with the Dominican Republic. Although the debts could not be accurately accounted for, they were legal because Dominican heads of state had forced the Dominican Congress to approve them. Hollander indicated that two alternative plans for retiring the debt had been submitted to Federico Velázquez, the Dominican treasury minister. One was the creditors' plan, which involved bringing the important creditors together and asking them to be party to the refinancing of the debt. The other called for raising money through a new loan negotiated for the most favorable terms possible to allow a settlement with all the creditors on a cash basis.

Cáceres sent Velázquez as special commissioner to work with Hollander, now employed as an agent of the Dominican government, to raise the money to refinance the debt. The two men developed an adjustment plan whereby the debt was reduced from US$40,269,404 to US$17,000,000. The government's earlier claim that its debts amounted to only US$29,020,393 was ignored. Hollander then proposed a US$20,000,000 loan, guaranteed by the U.S. government, from Kuhn, Loeb and Company of New York. Hollander summarized the deal as follows:

> (1) An agreement with Kuhn, Loeb and Co., of New York, for the issue and sale, at 96, of bonds of the Dominican Republic to the amount of $20,000,000, bearing 5 percent interest payable in fifty years, and redeemable after ten years at 102 1/2, and requiring payment of at least 1 percent per annum for amortization. The proceeds of the bonds, together with the funds segregated for the benefit of creditors under the interim arrangement, were to be applied first to the payment of the debts and claims as adjusted, second to the extension of certain burden-

some concessions and monopolies, and, to the construction under proper restrictions, of railroads, bridges, and other public improvements. ...

(2) An agreement with the Morton Trust Company of New York City to act (a) as depositary to receive the purchase price of the new bonds when paid and to encourage and promote the adjustment of the outstanding indebtedness and claims in accordance with the terms offered by the republic; and (b) as fiscal agent of the loan, to receive from out the customs revenues collected by the United States the sum of $100,000 monthly to be applied to the payment of interest upon and to the provision of a sinking fund for the new bonds. ...

(3) An offer settlement to the holders of recognized debts and claims, enumerated therein, to adjust these in cash at rates ranging, respectively, from 90 to 10 percent of the nominal values. ... The nominal aggregate of the recognized debts and claims included in the offer of settlement, exclusive of accrued interest, was $31,833,510, for which the republic proposed to pay in adjustment $5,526,240, together with certain interest correspondingly reduced. (U.S. Senate, 1907:291–292)

A commission composed of members of the Dominican Treasury Ministry and the Ministry of Foreign Relations was appointed to study the proposed Hollander-Velázquez agreement. It submitted an alternative plan to Congress on 29 April 1907, along with a critical report by Congressman M. de J. Aybar. According to this plan, the republic's public debt was to be consolidated and discharged with a new loan of only US$10,000,000. With a loan of US$20,000,000, it would take the country fifty years to pay off a total of US$46,503.15. Instead, if the nation's debt were reduced to US$10,000,000, the financial dependence of the country would last only twelve to thirteen years, and the country would pay US$14,255,248 in principal and interest. (Aybar opposed that part of the commission's plan that called for public works, for which over US$5,000,000 was allocated [Herrera, 1955, Document No. 32:408–446]). Congress rejected this proposal (partly because of Cáceres's political subordination to the United States) and accepted the Hollander-Velázquez contract.

Although the Hollander-Velázquez agreement meant a significant reduction in Dominican foreign and local debt, the change of creditors was part of a still-broader process that established the foundation for a subordinated state. The new deal benefited New York bankers, who made a good profit through the consolidation of debts that Hollander himself had said were not credible. Hollander profited greatly as well; he received US$100,000 from the Dominican government for his services, in addition to the US$40,000 that his own government paid him. Dominican debts were consolidated, but the Dominican state had lost its sovereignty by allowing a foreign power to control its finances.

Kuhn, Loeb and Company and the Morton Trust Company conditioned their participation in the refinancing of the debt on the signing of a Dominican-American convention whereby the United States would directly collect the customs revenues of the Dominican Republic. The convention was ratified by the U.S. Senate and the Dominican Congress and was signed on 25 July 1907. It declared that that political disturbances by both regular and revolutionary governments had led to the creation of debts and claims, many of doubtful validity in whole or in part, that amounted to over US$30,000,000 (nominal value). It indicated that the Dominican government had

> effected a conditional adjustment and settlement of said debts and claims under which all its foreign creditors have agreed to accept about $12,407,000 for debts and claims amounting to about $21,184,000 nominal or face value, and the holders of internal debts or claims of about $2,028,258, and the remaining holders of internal debts or claims on the same basis. ... the debt is reduced to ... more than $17,000,000. (Convention, 1910:307–310)

The president of the United States appointed a general receiver of Dominican customs to collect all customs duties. This general receiver was to act in accordance with the plan of adjustment with Kuhn, Loeb and Company of New York and to receive from the U.S. government "such protection as it may find to be requisite." The Dominican Republic had become a de facto protectorate of the United States, because this "protection" could easily be interpreted as military intervention to protect U.S. interests. Furthermore, the convention stipulated that "until the Dominican Republic has paid the whole amount of the bonds of the debt its public debt shall not be increased except by previous agreement between the Dominican Government and the United States" (Convention, 1910:307–310).

Conclusion

The Dominican-American Convention of 1907 was a landmark in the integration of Dominican finance into the international credit system. In contrast to previous debt arrangements with foreign creditors, it established a special relationship whereby the United States controlled the republic's purse strings. National plans for developing a locally led nation-state withered away. Local and foreign merchants were gradually marginalized from the mainstreams of government credit. Since the early 1890s the U.S.-based SDIC had administered Dominican customs and debts, and this relationship had proved fatal for the Dominican government. Under the interim agreement worked out with the U.S. government in 1905 to modernize Dominican customs, the collection of receipts had improved, but the nation-state had lost its sovereignty. The methods implemented in 1905 as an interim measure became, after 1907, legal measures that went so far as to regulate the state's accounting procedures and budget. The customs receivership was to develop and update its accounts in a regular manner. The government was to have a clearly defined budget that it could apportion among the various ministries. In addition, money was to be allocated to public works projects and to the development of a modern army and police force. These administrative mechanisms helped to build the modern Dominican state but barred local political elites from enjoying government largesse.

The Dominican-American Convention dealt a mortal blow to local and foreign merchants, bringing to an end the role they had been playing in Dominican economic history. Now they were forced to limit their activities to the import-export trade, an area tightly controlled by the United States, Germany, England, and Spain. The 1907 convention strengthened the state but weakened its local base of support.

4

The Beginnings of the Modern Dominican State

The dictatorship of Ulises Heureaux (1882–1899) and the regime of Ramón Cáceres (1906–1911) were, among other things, two distinct attempts to develop a state that could effectively organize political power and begin to create the conditions necessary for capital accumulation. Initially, Heureaux's dictatorship articulated the political and economic interests of an emerging bourgeoisie based on sugar planting and commerce. This national phase of state formation failed because of the monopolization of the sugar industry by U.S. corporations and dependence on foreign credit. Cáceres also made an effort to build a modern state, but his policies were inconsistent with national political and economic interests and simply subordinated local elites to the modernizing tendencies introduced by U.S. expansion into the Caribbean Basin.

Party Politics, Caudillo Politics, and State Formation

Whether Dominican political parties have historically been based on ideology and class is the subject of considerable debate. The Partido Rojo (Red Party) formed around Buenaventura Báez, had already declined significantly when Gregorio Luperón came to power in December 1879. Luperón inaugurated the era of the Partido Azul (Blue Party) by militarily defeating Báez's forces. Traditionally these parties, or more appropriately, political movements, have been depicted as polar opposites ideologically, with the Azules ostensibly following the liberal ideas of Juan Pablo Duarte and the Trinitarios, and the Rojos emphasizing annexation. The Partido Azul is usually characterized as composed of selfless nationalists. The most important intellectuals of the time, including Pedro Francisco Bonó, Ulises Francisco Espaillat, Father Fernando Antonio de Meriño, and Máximo Grullón joined its ranks. These prominent political figures advocated the development of a liberal democratic state modeled on the United States, France, and England. The Partido Rojo is generally described as a group of men lacking common ideals but fanatically following Báez, their caudillo.

Julio Campillo Pérez has described the social bases of the two parties as follows: The Partido Rojo was composed of (1) the *antisantanistas* of the First Republic, (2) many local caciques or regional caudillos, (3) much of the landowning and commercial sector, (4) most of the peasants and the poor, and (5) a small portion of the youth and professionals. The Partido Azul was composed of (1) the *neoduartistas*, (2) most of the old *santanistas*, (3) former *baecista* caciques and some local *santanistas*, (4) part of the commercial and landowning sectors, (5) most of the youth and intellectuals, (6) a small number of peasants and urban poor, and (7) "the bulk of the humble classes raised socially and politically by the Revolution" (Campillo Pérez, 1966:60).

According to Bosch, *baecismo* drew its strength from natural leaders of the populace originating in the lower petit bourgeoisie, particularly among the poor and very poor. The Partido Azul, in contrast, drew its constituency from middle and upper strata of the petit bourgeoisie, which had led the War of Restoration against Spain and shortly afterward had had to spend over ten years fighting Báez forces (Bosch, 1984:291–298). For Bosch the main contradictions and struggles occurred among the various strata of the late-nineteenth-century petit bourgeoisie. The question remains, however, whether there was any social, class, or ideological difference between the two political forces. It is generally accepted that the Partido Azul was nationalist and that the Partido Rojo was annexationist, but at times one finds annexationist or conservative elements among the Azules. President José María Cabral (1866–1868), for example, attempted to annex Samaná Bay to the United States, producing a brief division within the Azules and bringing about the downfall of his regime. Campillo Pérez finds the root of the differences between these two parties in the lack of a caudillo in the Partido Azul. The Rojo had one and thus responded more appropriately to the social circumstances of the country: "the emotional temperament of our people, combined with their limited political education, lent itself more to the dazzling man, despite his fraudulence or evil designs, than to a scattered group full of sincere and virtuous ideals" (Campillo Pérez, 1966:59–60). For Hoetink, however, the difference between these two political forces was not so clear.

> That only the rojos were "annexationists," as has sometimes been asserted, is difficult to prove. That the azules represented more liberal spirits is plausible up to a certain point, for the Cibao, where ... this party was strongly represented, counted among its political elite a number of men who by their education were strongly oriented toward Europe. The influence of cosmopolitan Hostos and of Betances on this group, Luperón included, should also be pointed out. In political practice, however, these lofty ideals had scant opportunity to be realized. ... The "doctors" depended upon the "generals," and the European-oriented intel-

lectual had to consider the available human material and the structure and culture peculiar to his country. (Hoetink, 1982:119)

It seems that though party leadership and ideological orientation may have a certain importance in explaining political behavior throughout the nineteenth and early twentieth centuries, strong caudillos structured political alliances. The Azules were unable to consolidate political power until Luperón's lieutenant Ulises Heureaux developed a political constituency in the south and east through patronage and bribes. After the War of Restoration, no Azul government lasted for any considerable period. Báez, in contrast, despite his failure to annex the country to a foreign power or arrange successful loans abroad, was the president five times. Ironically, he took power after his supporters had prepared the way for him: only when a government had been overthrown did he return from exile to take over the reins of government. He ruled with an iron hand and accepted no opposition within his ranks. The fact that he had left the country when Santana annexed it to Spain did not diminish his popularity. Why would significant sectors of the population support Báez when he did not seem to care enough about his country to endure hardship for it? Rufino Martínez provides this answer:

> The Dominican people are a conglomerate which needs a director of public opinion, or caudillo. When problems affecting their lives or destiny present themselves, in the absence of a collective consciousness to determine their point of view and push for a determined solution, they turn blindly to whatever occurs to their directors of opinion to say or do. Whatever occurs to him (the leader) is conveyed to them. This is how the annexation to Spain was accomplished.
>
> The Restoration War drew in all Dominicans, some in favor of their nation (independence), others against. The result was a copious harvest of generals and officers; and the rest of the men able to fight were also armed. Each region developed its own leaders, with a regional tint; there was no one leader behind whom the multitude of soldiers fought and behind whom the people would unite, giving obedience and support. The gregarious spirit of the people cannot exist without the caudillo: he is a resource without which the people are torpid, having to do for themselves much that they have never learned to do. At the end of the Santana Cycle, the society was very far from being able to advance alone. (Martínez, 1985:335–336)

Although caudillos did play a key role in structuring political alliances, it was not because of "the emotional temperament of the people" or the "absence of a collective consciousness" in the Dominican people. Caudillismo was the product of a weak and undeveloped society, itself the result of the lack of integration of the national economy. The society's dominant blocs were constituted not as a bourgeoisie but only as the embryo of such a class. Consequently, there was no unified ruling political elite capable of dominating national politics. Instead, regional caudillos took the place of a "national" elite.

Thus, the rivalries between caudillos and the wars that ensued expressed social conflicts that had not yet assumed the form of class struggle in the strict sense. This does not mean, however, that these political struggles had no class content. As we have seen, caudillos established political alliances with merchants who lent them money in exchange for reduced duties at the customs houses. After 1865 local and foreign merchants established credit associations that loaned money to caudillos both in and out of power. Similarly, caudillos sought to establish political connections with the pioneers of the sugar industry because many of them were also established local brokers. These alliances fueled the engine of caudillo politics and had an impact on the emergence of the state. Thus, the first political experience of the Dominican people could not transcend what Dominican society offered: the provincial rivalry and consequent disorder of caudillo politics.

The organization of caudillo political power in the post-Báez period required the creation of class-based alliances. Backed by Cibao merchants, Luperón and his Partido Azul were able to do this. From his Puerto Plata–based government, Luperón sent Ulises Heureaux to represent him in the south and east. Heureaux was already familiar with those regions, having participated in numerous battles against Báez's forces throughout the country. "He was the most appropriate man to develop the political alliances necessary," comments Juan Bosch, "because he had a thorough knowledge of the Dominican social reality, an acute natural intelligence, and a great capacity for action and reaction" (Bosch, 1988:51–52). Unlike Luperón, who seems to have been concerned with the development of liberal democratic institutions, Heureaux was a practical man. He continually complained about Luperón's idealism and often reproached him for not understanding the art of ruling. Heureaux seemed to understand clearly the need to establish politico-economic as well as narrowly political alliances.

Heureaux was a pragmatic politician. He once wrote that "with regard to politics, I have no loves. I follow a course to reach the attainment of my goal. ... I will gather up men where I find them, I will appraise them, and I will treat them considerately in accord with the conduct that they follow with me" (Hoetink, 1982:130). Armed with this opportunistic view of politics, he was able to build political alliances beyond the requirements of his assignment.

Heureaux Versus De Moya

Two important political victories helped Heureaux: the defeat of a Cibao-based rebellion led by Casimiro Nemecio de Moya and the political break with Luperón. These victories were made possible by the alliances he had established with the pioneers of the sugar industry and with merchants. Strengthened by them, he set out to build a nation-state responsive to national political interests.

When Heureaux reached the presidency of the republic for the first time in 1882, he was no newcomer to politics: he had been exercising great political power behind the scenes as minister of the interior since 1880. He encountered no significant difficulties during his first administration (1882–1884) and did not object to Francisco G. Billini's taking office at the end of his term because he thought Billini would let him pull the strings unofficially. Under pressure from Heureaux, Billini resigned in 1885, and Alejandro Woos y Gil (1885–1886) succeeded him. Woos y Gil was of course a mere figurehead controlled by Heureaux. Heureaux's efforts did not go unchallenged, however. Resistance came from within the ranks of his own Partido Azul. The Cibao-based general Casimiro Nemecio de Moya claimed that Heureaux had used regional caciques to engineer the fraudulent election of Billini. This accusation created much bitterness among the Azules and eventually led to Billini's resignation in 1885. Many Cibao-based merchants and farmers felt that Heureaux was neglecting their political and economic interests, and De Moya began expressing their indignation. Having gathered political support in La Vega, Santiago, Puerto Plata, and even Santo Domingo, he used it to launch his own candidacy in the 1886 presidential elections. Heureaux had been working hard to obtain the support of prestigious former *baecistas* like Eugenio Generoso de Marchena, Manuel María Gautier, and Braulio Alvarez. The Rojos had disappeared with Báez's death, and Heureaux had little difficulty drawing them into the conservative wing of the Azul party. Luperón had trouble accepting these conservatives, but, to the displeasure of some young Cibao liberals, he did support Heureaux in the 1886 presidential elections, (Martínez, 1971:264–265).

These elections were the acid test of a Cibao-based challenge to Heureaux's political power and proved both highly competitive and violent. The U.S. consul in Santo Domingo reported to the State Department that "great political excitement prevails for the coming presidential and vice-presidential elections. ... The competition is alarming because of the abusive language used by both parties. ... A lot of people fear a revolution." The French consul reported that "it was evident to everyone that the government favored General Heureaux. The government exercised a certain pressure over the population. ... De Moya's party refused to vote in the last few days and declared that it was going to protest before the nation" (Domínguez, 1986:18–19).

Heureaux claimed victory, but the election results were not immediately published. He sent Woos y Gil to La Vega to negotiate with De Moya, but instead, De Moya declared war. The rebellion lasted for three months, and various accounts of it report nearly six hundred dead and wounded. In spite of Luperón's open support for Heureaux, De Moya's followers initially took a number of towns and were ready to march on Santo Domingo. Heureaux, however, wasted no time in traveling to Puerto Plata to request a loan of US$80,000 from the Spanish merchant Cosme Batlle. Apparently Batlle did not have the sum himself but raised the money from other Spanish merchants in the city (Domínguez, 1986:21). In exchange he was granted a duty-free award in the Puerto Plata customs house, which allowed him and other foreign merchants to save a fortune in duties. Meanwhile, Heureaux headed for Santiago and distributed money among De Moya's followers throughout the Cibao. Even Benito Monción, one of the rebellion's greatest generals, succumbed to Heureaux's bribery, and soon afterward, the insurrection collapsed (Martínez, 1971:231).

As we have seen, the merchants and the sugar producers had developed an alliance with Heureaux, whereas De Moya relied for support on the Cibao tobacco farmers and medium-sized merchants. Thus political struggles seemingly based only on personal ties and the authoritarian personality of a caudillo had a regional character that involved economic issues.

Heureaux Versus Luperón

Luperón had become a very wealthy man and increasingly perceived himself as above national political struggles. Although still active in the Partido Azul, he devoted more time to his commercial activities and travels in Europe. Meanwhile, Heureaux was working to assume control of the liberal forces that Luperón claimed to represent and lead. The political split between these two national leaders was partly due to the economic and political changes of the latter part of the nineteenth century, and it mirrored the Latin American political reality of the time. Former liberals such as Porfirio Díaz in Mexico, and Justo Rufino Barrio in Guatemala had turned into conservative dictators. These dictators reflected the power of landed and merchant elites who had benefited from capitalist expansion as did Heureaux.

Heureaux had gained the support of Luperón in fighting De Moya, but thereafter their political differences became more pronounced. On the eve of his political break with Luperón, he wrote to a friend:

> The General (Luperón) does not want to understand that our situations are not identical, given that I assume the moral and material responsibilities of the Government, being the target of the shots from the intransigents from all the circles of my personal adversaries and from impertinent, ungrateful conspirators, while they only search out him who today finds himself more distant from public matters, when they want him to sponsor them and to guarantee them with the arrière-pensée of his falling out with me. ... You know him and know that for him there is neither law nor procedure except what his heart dictates, and no, no, it cannot be that way, the scripture teaches us that Cain killed his brother Abel. Why? Out of envy! And Abel was esteemed for being good. (Hoetink, 1982:130)

Heureaux was acutely aware that Luperón enjoyed wide popular support and might run for president in 1888. In addition, he knew that if the economic situation of the country continued to deteriorate his cash-starved government would be unable to offer patronage jobs to his political supporters. Direct popular elections would be inconvenient for him, particularly if Luperón decided to run. Thus, shortly after taking power in 1886 he began to develop a fallback position.

During the First Republic, presidential elections were indirect. The Partido Azul had opposed the exclusion of the masses from electoral politics, and once in power it had instituted universal suffrage and direct election of the president. Circumstances had changed, however, now that the Partido Azul had split and Heureaux headed its conservative wing. In a well-orchestrated political maneuver, Heureaux had his supporters in Cibao, De Moya's stronghold, call for indirect elections. In June 1887 a petition signed by leading political figures asserted that universal suffrage and direct elections were the cause of civil wars. In a related tactic, a congressional commission noted in October that political instability discredited the republic abroad and recommended the extension of the presidential term from two to four years (Domínguez, 1986:38–42). These alterations seemed acceptable to a significant segment of the population; on the surface there was no intrigue aimed at blocking Luperón's participation in the presidential race. Luperón had been charging Heureaux with corruption, and in September 1887 Heureaux responded:

> I do not venture to reply to your ideas regarding the system of Government that you say I have introduced; I believe that you knew that before my coming to public affairs, the country was dominated by corruption, and if I am not mistaken, it was the virus that infected the masses to overthrow the Government of Don Ulises (Espaillat); and as the country has continued under the sway of those same customs, in the Provisional Government you had to invent the expedient of asignaciones [patronage jobs] to divide the sums that are distributed in gifts and valuables more equitably. By continuing that order of affairs, it has become corrupt to the point that everyone wants to live off the State, and you, when you have been in power, have distributed considerable sums for the same purpose, but since you have not had the necessity of materially assuming the responsibility for these acts that you condemn, you blame me and accuse me without reflecting for a moment that the Republic has been turned topsy-turvy by others and that I have come to govern, finding it in chaos. (Hoetink, 1982:83)

A break between the two leaders was clearly imminent. Although he had the government apparatus at his disposal, Heureaux was not sure that he could defeat Luperón at the polls or even militarily. Luperón was not De Moya; he still enjoyed great military and political prestige. Heureaux did not mention that he was going to run in the 1888 elections when in November 1887 he arranged for Congress to approve the creation of two institutions to organize indirect elections: primary assemblies and an electoral council. The primary assemblies, locally elected bodies, were to choose delegates to represent their districts on the electoral council that would elect the president and the vice president.

There were two additional issues that Heureaux had to address before declaring his intention to seek reelection: the position of other prominent leaders within the Partido Azul and the gradual deterioration of the economy. His correspondence with various political friends shows him clearly maneuvering to gain political support. Responding to General Miguel Pichardo in June 1887, he wrote: "I wish to retire from office but I think that it is necessary first for me to know whose camp I should join." He complained to another friend that he was ill and needed to retire (Ortíz, 1975a:243). Although he told his close political allies that he was not sure about running, he encouraged Luperón to run because he "had more titles than any other citizen, excelling in merits." At the same time, he secretly asked that "all those who are my real friends and who believe in me that they not commit themselves even to Christ" because "as yet I do not see things clearly with respect to our interests and their security and to that of my friends in general" (Ortíz, 1975a:244). Heureaux perceived that a political group was in power, and he made this economic and political elite conscious of itself. In exchange for their loyalty, they were to receive government concessions and patronage jobs or subsidies. This policy further strained a government that was already cash-starved, because Heureaux's local creditors charged high interest rates.

Beginning in 1884 the Dominican economy faced new difficulties. The governor of Azua, General José D. Pichardo, complained in August 1887 that depreciation of local products in the international market was the cause of unemployment and misery in his province. Various sugar planters had gone out of business, and artisans as well as local merchants faced bankruptcy. In March 1888 the French vice consul in Santo Domingo described the economy as depressed, writing, "Public employees have not received their salaries for four or five months. The other day, before starting a new Congress, deputies demanded from the government their salaries for the past few months. They threatened to return to their provinces if their claims were not satisfied" (Domínguez, 1986:48–49).

By 1887 Heureaux knew that he could no longer depend on local and foreign merchants to save him as they had in 1886. They were charging 10–12 percent interest on loans, and in 1887 the government had to pay them 25 percent of its income. When the Westendorp loan came up for discussion in Congress, these merchants protested, and so did Luperón and the liberals of the Partido Azul, who considered it unacceptable to place the country's sovereignty in the hands of a foreign government.

The Westendorp loan did not generate enough funding to solve the economic problems Heureaux faced, but for a while the circulation of 3 million Spanish pesos satisfied local and foreign resident creditors and ameliorated the economy's ills. Heureaux took advantage of this conjuncture to announce his candidacy for president. In a 30 June 1888 letter to Juan Antonio Lora, he wrote:

> On this occasion, I firmly believe that my humble person is a necessity for peace; I say this because I am convinced that neither General Luperón nor any other political entity in the Republic has at its disposition the elements for peace as well as for turbulence which I can command; and, convinced of this as I am, the man who directs this country's politics and, to a certain extent, understands the way of thinking of the important men across the Republic, I need to make no declaration of faith in order to give them the confidence which they seek. (Ortíz, 1975a:245)

Nevertheless, Heureaux kept on encouraging Luperón to run for office. He went to Puerto Plata and signed an agreement with Luperón whereby the government guaranteed the right of the people to vote and pledged not to exert pressure on citizens to vote for the incumbent. As in 1884, however, he was prepared to do the opposite of what he had promised. A campaign of repression was unleashed nationwide against Luperón's supporters, and a number of political activists were arrested. When he learned that Luperón enjoyed wide support in Monte Cristi, Heureaux secretly advised its governor not to worry because in the Dominican Republic one ruled not by sympathy but by force. The general elections were scheduled for 1–2 November 1888. One week before the vote, Luperón withdrew from the race. He wrote:

> The Citizen President of the Republic made a pact with me, publicly known, to respect and cause to be respected the right of free suffrage enforcing the strictest legality upon the elections. It is with the utmost surprise that it has come to my knowledge and conviction that this accord has not been respected ... to the extreme that in Samaná, Matanzas, Moca, and other areas, by means of force the authorities have dissolved the committee, jailing some and persecuting others of their members. (Ortíz, 1975a:247)

Once Luperón had withdrawn, Heureaux had no opposition, and the campaign ended in victory for Heureaux.

The division with Luperón signaled the end of any prospects for the Cibao-based elites to control national political power. Having arranged negotiations with the Hartmont bondholders, Heureaux opened a new line of credit with Westendorp that reduced his responsiveness to merchants and sugar planters. His victories against De Moya and Luperón gave him breathing space to expand his political power base and begin organizing a bureaucracy to run the government and to strengthen the armed forces.

Expansion of the Power Base

Heureaux's strategy for expanding his power base to include traditional political elites involved paying attention to national political and economic interests. Aware of their social and political potential, he sought to cultivate a relationship with them through a program of government concessions. Helen Ortíz has compiled the following selected list:

> (1) Concession to E. G. de Marchena and others, March 12, 1980, to exploit a gold mine in San José de las Matas; (2) Concession to José Gabriel García (ex-Cabinet member) and Manuel de Jesús Rodríguez (Congressman), June 15, 1891, to build an iron bridge over Haina River; (3) Concession to Justice Minister Tomás Morales, May 13, 1892, to build a market in Higüey; (4) Concession to Governor Pedro Pepín of Santiago, April 23, 1892, to install a streetcar on government land in Santiago; (5) Concession to Arturo Damirón, Member of the Santo Domingo Ayuntamiento (Municipal Government), June 23, 1892, to build and maintain aqueducts in Santo Domingo and San Pedro de Macorís for fifty years; (6) Concession to Congressman Santelises, June 23, 1892, to establish a chain of soap factories throughout the Cibao; (7) Concession to Evaristo Demorizi (Government Delegate in Samaná), for a coconut oil factory in Samaná; (8) Concession to ex-President Billini, June 22, 1894, to establish telephone lines in the south and east with the center in San Pedro de Macorís; (9) Concession to Jorge Curiel (President of Congress), July 16, 1894, for Puerto Plata aqueduct construction and maintenance; (10) Concession to Congressman Hipólito Pierret to establish ice factories in Puerto Plata and Santiago; (11) Concession to Justice Minister S. Valverde for Santiago aqueduct. (Ortíz, 1975a:171–172)

Concessions were generally granted to create the necessary infrastructure for services and industries that responded to the needs of emerging towns, and those receiving them were identified with Heureaux and the political group in power. As noted earlier, Puerto Plata merchants received duty-free awards to introduce goods into the country, and sugar planters received concessions to import machinery for the construction of mills, railroads, and the like. Further, the regional political leaders were subsidized by Heureaux in exchange for their political support. The implementation of these policies strengthened Heureaux's regime but also greatly increased its class content.

Heureaux also had a clear vision of the role of the state in economic development. The first tenet of his pragmatic political philosophy was that economic progress had to be achieved in the Dominican Republic and that this progress depended on attracting foreign capital and expertise. The second tenet was that economic progress depended on peace and internal political stability. The third and key point was that the state should be the agent for bringing about economic growth and the internal climate needed for it; therefore, it had to take responsibility for the maintenance of peace and political stability at all costs. For Heureaux, the central government had to be strong politically and militarily in order to direct the nation's economic progress (Ortíz, 1975a:155–156).

State Power and Its Limitations

The integration of the Dominican Republic into the international capitalist system brought social and economic transformations that had a direct impact on the development of the state but prevented local elites from developing a strong economic base. As we have seen, investments in the sugar industry engendered an embryonic bourgeoisie, but the monopolization of the industry inhibited the process. Similarly, although local and foreign merchants had begun to form an indigenous merchant sector, reliance on foreign credit obstructed their full development as a merchant class.

Heureaux seems to have been intuitively aware that liberal democracy could not be implemented in the Dominican Republic because the country lacked the material basis for it. He believed that only force could produce political power and that money was necessary for political stability. Having defeated Luperón and the liberal wing of the Partido Azul, he considered it absolutely necessary to strengthen and professionalize the armed forces.

Under Heureaux, for the first time since Santana the Dominican Republic had a strong military caudillo who commanded national respect. His military and political skills were influential in the campaign to reorganize the army, but the developments of the forces of production brought about by capitalism played the key role. Since 1884 the state had had a telegraph system that was extensively used by the military. During the 1890s various important ports and cities (Santo Domingo, San Pedro de Macorís, Sánchez, Puerto Plata, Monte Cristi, Santiago, and others) had gained access to the telegraph. Prior to Heureaux no president had had such modern means of communication at his disposal. Heureaux developed a telegraph code for transmitting secret orders to military governors (Sang, 1989:78–82) and used the new means of communication to put down rebellions. In November 1888 U.S. Consul H.C.C. Astwood reported on the method Heureaux had used to stifle a rebellion in Puerto Plata before it started: "The news was telegraphed here and in 48 hours everything was organized for a vigorous campaign; the movements of General Heureaux were so rapid that it caused a complete stamped(e) to those who had pretended to side with the revolutionaries and the whole thing collapsed without the firing of a shot" (Ortíz, 1975a:196). Telephones were installed in Santo Domingo in 1886, and in 1893 private lines were installed for communicating with the sugar plantations. In the 1890s the most important military fortress was wired for telephone service. These new means of communication helped the army become an important agent of political stabilization and domination.

Although modern roads did not yet connect important cities, the first railroad was completed in 1887, linking the port of Sánchez to the interior city of La Vega, 130 kilometers distant. Railroads, a by-product of capitalist penetration, were also used by the military. Heureaux was able to move troops from either Sánchez or Puerto Plata to control the whole Cibao. The ability to move ground troops rapidly by railroad was supplemented by the development of the Dominican navy. In 1882 the navy had consisted of one small ship owned by Juan Bautista Vicini that the government occasionally used. During the late 1880s the government bought the gunboat the *Presidente* and ordered the construction of two more, the *Independencia,* and the *Restauración.* In 1893 Congress approved the purchase of another steamer, the *16 de Agosto.* For the first time troops could be moved rapidly to the Cibao by sea.

The army was a key factor in shaping the national unity of the state as an instrument of stabilization and political domination. In his inaugural speech in 1882 Heureaux said, "there is a widely held belief that it is possible to govern without an army; I, too, would hold it if those who opposed the government did not exceed peaceful limits. But as the opposition in our country is in inverse relation to the material power of the government ... [the army] is indispensable" (Ortíz, 1975a:211). From 1882 on, a standing army and a conscription system were developed. More than any other group, the peasantry was subject to conscription; many urban residents avoided conscription by bribing the authorities. The formal mechanisms for buying matériel did not work effectively, thus Heureaux had to take care of the smallest details:

> He oversaw the purchase of armaments and personally wrote a letter of complaint to the supplier of this same equipment in Liege; he even gave orders for taking the measurements of a second lieutenant for his uniform. Before undertaking a trip to a remote region of the country, he maintained correspondence about the equipment of the soldiers who were to accompany him, requesting that they let him know by telegraph if there were not enough shoes. In short, he was vigilant, and he gave practical advice: Take special care for me with troops of Samaná ... teaching them to keep their clothes clean and to use and shine shoes. It is necessary to drill them in military exercises with all the firmness necessary. (Hoetink, 1982:102)

Clearly, Heureaux's army was not a modern one, and this explains his paternalism. "General Lilís [Heureaux], when he had the chance to visit that Corps, said to them in greeting, 'How are you, my sons?' To which, very happy, they replied with the greatest affection, 'Very well, dear papa.'" Although these troops were "*la flor y nata*" [the elite] of the army, their loyalty was first to the caudillo and only then to the military code (Bueno, 1961:299–300).

By 1899 Heureaux had established forces in Santo Domingo, Santiago, Azua, Moca, Samaná, La Vega, Puerto Plata, San Francisco de Macorís, Monte Cristi, and San Pedro de Macorís. Summarizing the condition of the armed forces for one of his closest generals in 1897, he wrote:

With the help of God we continue to advance. We now have a quite disciplined army; fourteen thousand Remington rifles with more than three million bullets are deposited in our arsenals; we have six artillery batteries, high-caliber for use in the mountains. ... all equipped with the corresponding supplies and munitions; and the flag of the Republic now flies above three rapid steam-powered warships valued at two million pesos, armed with thirty pieces of the best artillery. Moreover, rail lines have been built, giving strategic advantages, and will permit, along with the fleet, the rapid deployment of our forces, (Ortíz, 1975a:214)

The army was responsive to one national caudillo. Congress was controlled by the conservative wing of Heureaux's political party, and therefore it was not difficult for him to have it approve all the necessary contracts to integrate Dominican finance into the international credit system. In effect, Congress served only to provide a veil of legality for Heureaux's dictatorship rather than to act as a counterbalance to the executive.

Heureaux was well aware of his decisive role within the emerging Dominican state. He knew, or sensed, that he could not fully count on any of the so-called government institutions, such as Congress or the courts. Although he spent a great deal of time and energy developing a strong army loyal to himself, he did not consider it the key to consolidating political power. For him, money was the key to keeping his government machine running. In 1882, in his capacity as minister of the interior, he had written: "the only thing that satisfies our people is money; nothing else is spoken of; no one serves if it is not for money .... Due to ... money we have peace and, without it, this will not be maintained. If they do not advance us that power agent, all is risked: peace, Government and Capital (Ortíz, 1975a:168). Experience had taught Heureaux that at times pesos were more effective than bullets. When he confronted the largest Cibao-based rebellion in 1886, rather than mounting a huge military operation, he went to Puerto Plata to borrow money from merchants to buy off the most effective of the rebellion's generals. His correspondence shows that he had loyal but paid informers in every city or town of the republic who kept him abreast of the political movements of the opposition. Their support, however, cost the government dearly.

Government spending nearly tripled from 1887 to 1893, from 35,000 pesos to 90,000 pesos monthly. Meanwhile, the prices of Dominican exports were falling. The sugar industry suffered another significant slowdown in 1893, and the price of tobacco had been declining in Germany since the beginning of the decade. This meant a significant reduction in government income at the same time that political demands forced larger government expenditures. Consequently, Heureaux had less money to maintain the subsidies for his pool of informers. The control of the state's income first by Westendorp and then by the SDIC reduced his ability to maintain his political support, and this helped prepare the way for the emergence of new political forces. Social and political conditions deteriorated as the Dominican economy was engulfed by the international capitalist system, and the pioneers of the sugar industry were steadily driven out of business. Local and foreign merchants as well as sugar planters had seen their income reduced when the government handed over control to the SDIC. In this context the state's customs houses and foreign loans had become cherished sources of revenue. To regain control of their nation, local elites sought ways of overthrowing Heureaux.

The crisis created by Heureaux's economic policy led to an armed revolt in 1889. The Fanita expedition was led by Juan Isidro Jiménes, whose relations with Heureaux had been excellent until he had developed an interest in politics. In the summer of 1899 Jiménes sailed from Mobile, Alabama, to organize a guerrilla force in Monte Cristi. The expedition was a military failure, and many of Jiménes's followers were killed. Jiménes himself was lucky to escape with his life (Sang, 1989:180–186; Domínguez, 1986:230–234). His crusade nevertheless expressed the discontent of local political elites and their opposition to the dictatorship. As we have seen, Heureaux's inflationary policies had gradually alienated the merchants and sugar planters who had already had their incomes reduced by his reliance on foreign credit; when he tried to stem inflation by burning the inflated bills, it was already too late.

Foreign credit enabled Heureaux to enjoy relative autonomy from merchants and planters, but it subordinated the state to foreign banks by increasing the foreign debt. He was able to centralize the armed forces with the aid of new means of transport and communications and develop a government bureaucracy, and under his leadership the Dominican state became an agent of economic growth and capitalist development. In this sense, his dictatorship represented an initial step in the development of a modern state. This development was, however, delayed by the new form of integration of the Dominican state into the international capitalist system, which demanded a state that was responsive not just to one man but to its local and foreign obligations. The combination of the regime's political incapacity to live up to these new expectations, the struggles of the remnants of the embryonic bourgeoisie, and the government's inflationary policies led the dictatorship into a crisis that ended in its downfall.

The Modern State and the U.S. Semiprotectorate

Heureaux's assassination in 1899 marked the beginning of a period of political instability and a near collapse of government institutions. However, the social and economic structure of the Dominican Republic had been radically altered. The development of the emerging bourgeoisie based on sugar planting and commerce had been cut off. The political forces competing for political power were the remnants of a class that had failed to become a national bourgeoisie. These political groupings sought to control state power, which was the main source of revenue left to them. Because they were politically weak and incapable of structuring national political organizations, rivalry among caudillos returned to the Dominican political process.

Twentieth-century caudillo rivalries were conditioned by U.S. interventionist policy. The negotiations conducted with the United States over the Dominican debt illustrate the dynamic of caudillo political struggles. As has been noted, the struggles for the spoils of government office and the conflictual relationship with the SDIC led to a division between Vásquez and Jiménes in April 1902, allowing Woos y Gil, a former Heureaux ally, to take over the government. Vásquez and Jiménes worked together to overthrow Woos y Gil in November 1903, and a compromise candidate, Carlos Morales Languasco, assumed the presidency. Cáceres, a member of Vásquez's inner circle, was appointed to the vice presidency as part of a political strategy designed to reduce the president's power.

The interim agreement that Morales Languasco reached with the United States in 1905 provided for the United States to establish and administer a customs receivership in the name of the Dominican government. Morales Languasco was forced to negotiate this, however, with Monte Cristi's caudillos, Andrés Navarro, Demetrio Rodríguez, and Desiderio Arias (Jiménes Grullón, 1975:138), and he decided to appoint Arias military governor of the province (a concession that included control of the Monte Cristi customs house). Cáceres, dissatisfied because this gave Monte Cristi political autonomy, gradually began to act independently of the president and to solicit the support of the cabinet. When Morales Languasco failed to save himself through a coup, Cáceres assumed the presidency.

The Cáceres regime (1906–1911) represented a second phase in the development of a modern Dominican state. U.S. sugar corporations and banks had nearly replaced foreign resident sugar planters and merchants in the country's economic mainstream. The U.S. government backed Cáceres when he undertook projects that promised to retire foreign debt or to create an infrastructure that would benefit U.S. sugar concerns on the island. In fact, it was under Cáceres that the Dominican-American Convention was signed in 1907. Increases in Dominican traditional exports, reduction and consolidation of internal and external debts, and the implementation of strict methods for collecting customs duties allowed his regime a degree of political stability. These circumstances helped him to launch a program that provided the order required by U.S. regional political, economic, and military interests in the Caribbean Basin. With U.S. support, Cáceres expanded military control across the nation's territory, took the first steps toward the establishment of a professional constabulary separate from the traditional caudillos, introduced legislation to further the development of modern capitalist property, and implemented a system of public works.

Cáceres's power base, unlike that of Heureaux, was not national. By signing the 1907 convention he turned the Dominican state into a semiprotectorate of the United States. Early in his administration, Cáceres reassured foreign political backers that he was willing and able to exercise military control across the national territory. When he took power in 1906 he became personally involved in "pacifying" the northeastern region, politically and militarily controlled by Arias. In return for loans to finance his rebellion against Morales Languasco, Arias had allowed merchants to pay reduced tariffs. Importers preferred to unload at the port of Monte Cristi even if their products were destined for Santo Domingo or San Pedro de Macorís because of Arias's duty discounts (Domínguez, 1988). Arias expected an appointment from the Cáceres regime, but Cáceres declined to negotiate with him. In September 1906, Cáceres left Santo Domingo on a German merchant ship bound for Monte Cristi with one thousand soldiers and declared martial law in the northeastern region. When a deadline established for the surrender of the rebels had passed, he dispatched his soldiers all over the region to look for Arias's guerrillas. Much as General Valeriano Weyler had in his campaign against the Mambises in Cuba, Cáceres ordered his troops to kill all the cattle that wandered the region, seeking to eliminate all sources of food so that the guerrillas would be forced to surrender or face starvation. The devastation was so "huge that for a long time the northeastern region was deserted; it was not possible to count on natural resources to sustain guerrilla warfare" (Troncoso Sánchez, 1964:265). Arias, acknowledging defeat, went into exile.

The military defeat of Arias allowed Cáceres to concentrate on the consolidation of his regime. He began to buy weapons to improve the firepower of the army while reorganizing the battalions created by Heureaux. He also ordered the restructuring of the police force that Morales Languasco had founded. This new republican guard was intended to take power away from local caciques. According to Sumner Welles, these two forces were the best the country had ever had:

> The organization of the armed forces of the Republic, which were now for the first time in the history of the nation decently fed and clothed, and promptly paid, made it difficult for any rebellion to meet with success, in particular since the President's personal popularity throughout the country was so great that a rebellion could scarcely hope for more than purely local response. (Welles, 1928:667)

This reorganization was part of a general legislative program mandated by the Constitution of 1908, which sought to structure a modern state. The Constitution of 1908 was a landmark in the development of the modern Dominican state. Since 1844 constitutional reforms had been used by various caudillos to establish themselves in power. Báez and Santana had made extensive use of this mechanism during the First Republic, and from 1866 to 1879 ten different governments had introduced reforms, none of which affected the substance of the original constitution. Under Heureaux, Congress had approved two important constitutional reforms, reintroducing indirect elections and extending the presidential term from two to four years. In 1896 the constitution was recast to include reelection of the president; like previous reforms, this one was designed to strengthen the power of the executive. In contrast, the Constitutional Assembly of 1908 was made up of prominent lawyers and citizens with a degree of independence from the executive. They took the U.S. Constitution as a model and therefore envisioned a strong executive. The new constitution restructured the cabinet, creating ministers of state without responsibility to Congress. It extended the presidential term to six years and eliminated the vice presidency. In an effort to eliminate traditional caudillismo and caciquismo, it substituted the post of military governor for that of civil governor and placed both above all other authorities, military and judicial. Military tasks remained in the hands of "professionally" trained officers.

Since 1879 Congress had had only one chamber. The reforms of 1908 provided for a Cámara de Diputados (Lower House) and a Cámara de Senadores (Senate). The Lower House was empowered to impeach the president and the members of the Supreme Court. It approved or rejected contracts agreed upon by municipal governments and authorized Dominican citizens to take public office. The Senate appointed the members of the Supreme Court and the members of the Auditing Board and considered the Lower House's impeachment of the president. In theory, these duties enhanced the power of Congress to serve as a counterbalance to a strong executive.

The judiciary was also enlarged and strengthened. The Supreme Court was empowered to declare whether a law was constitutional and to supervise the conduct of all judicial employees. The constitution provided for the creation of two additional courts of appeal and required a law degree as a qualification for a judgeship (Mejía, 1976:57–66).

The framers of the 1908 Constitution ensured the liberal democratic character of the modern Dominican state. They were aware, however, that the social and political conditions of Dominican society did not correspond to the new charter, and therefore gave the president absolute power to control the executive. This was a blank check for Ramón Cáceres, who was elected president in 1908 with no apparent opposition.

Cáceres seemed to understand that formal restructuring of the state by the constitution was insufficient to separate the caudillos from politics. He created a special account in the budget "for Generals accountable to the President." These "generals" were the warriors who supported the leading caudillos of the time, Jiménes and Vásquez, and the fund granted them a sort of pension in exchange for political neutrality. When these "generals" declined to retire, Cáceres sent them out of their regions, thus increasing the political strength of the army (Moya Pons, 1981:450).

Dominicans had framed a constitution that in theory strengthened the liberal democratic state. In practice, however, this state had become a semiprotectorate of the United States and rather than legislating to protect local elites, Cáceres protected the new corporate owners of the Dominican sugar plantations.

His fiscal policy exempted sugar corporations from taxes on the import of machinery and on the export of their produce. His legislation allowed for the partition of communal lands, thus giving the sugar corporations a free hand to expand onto the best land in the region. At the same time he imposed taxes on local businessmen and producers of other products, and this type of legislation eventually produced an effective opposition to his regime.

Public works projects were high on the Cáceres agenda. In accordance with the Hollander-Velázquez plan of adjustment, the Dominican government had received US$500,000 for public works. A bureau of public works was created and a U.S. engineer appointed as its director. Significant improvements were made in the areas of public sanitation, reconstruction of piers, and highway construction:

> The highroad by which it was intended to link the capital with Azua was completed within a brief period as far as the town of San Cristobal, and the northern highroad, destined to connect the capital with the cities of the Cibao, was completed during these years so far as Los Alcarrizos. The roads thus constructed under the supervision of an American Chief Engineer were high grade roads intended to withstand the heavy traffic which it was believed would shortly develop. (Welles, 1928:665)

The Puerto Plata–Santiago line was extended to Moca and inaugurated on 24 October 1909. Plans were made to extend the rail lines to La Vega, Cotuí, and Santo Domingo and to link Santiago and Monte Cristi.

Cáceres's policies were procapitalist and classist in that they favored foreign sugar corporations, bankers, and a small sector of the local political elite while excluding the popular sectors from political power and government largesse. These policies generated considerable resentment both within Cáceres's party and outside it. Local brokers were not at all pleased with the arrangements made with the New York bankers, nor were the Vásquez followers who had been left out of the distribution of patronage jobs. To deflect some of this anger, Cáceres placed Federico Velázquez in charge of the Treasury Ministry and Alfredo Victoria in charge of the army.

Despite Cáceres's attempts to avoid blame, Vásquez's supporters continued to charge that the president had betrayed them. Vásquez had been in charge of the Central Dominican Railroad, and when he learned that the government was speculating with lands seized to build the railroad and that Velázquez was involved in the affair, he resigned and left for Europe.

In a private letter to Cáceres that apparently never reached him, Vásquez complained that his economic policy had caused suffering to the majority of the Dominican people and aroused inchoate but persistent and powerful dissatisfaction. He urged Cáceres not to use repression against the legitimate demands of the people. Reconciliation would be impossible if one branch of government (here he implicitly referred to Velázquez's Ministry of Hacienda) acted with absolute independence and was allowed to monopolize the administration of public affairs (Welles, 1928:670–672). When Vásquez learned of the plot to assassinate Cáceres, he distanced himself from any plans to overthrow the government. Nonetheless, the plotting continued and Cáceres was assassinated in 1911. This assassination, like Heureaux's, unleashed political forces that had been excluded from political power.

Although the Constitution of 1908 provided for a balance of power between the executive and legislative branches, the former tended to grow more and more powerful. A weak Congress and an "overgrown" executive were due to a weak and regionally fragmented bourgeoisie. Alienated from the mainstream of the Dominican economy, local elites lacked the political might to counter a strong executive with political opposition in Congress.

Conclusion

Heureaux's attempt to developed a strong nation-state based on sugar planting and commerce failed in part because of the contradictory integration of the Dominican state into the international capitalist system and the socioeconomic weakness of the bourgeoisie that supported him. His failures led to increasing U.S. involvement in Dominican political and economic affairs. When Cáceres took power, the marginalization of the sugar elites and their replacement by U.S. corporations was complete, and his efforts to promote the sugar industry benefited foreign capital, not national businessmen.

Neither Heureaux nor Cáceres was able to develop stable political institutions capable of providing a peaceful transfer of power. In both cases the government was controlled by a strong executive; Congress existed only to lend a semblance of legality to an authoritarian state. Strong civic institutions could not develop because the pioneers of the sugar industry and the foreign merchants were excluded from the mainstream of the economy just when they were beginning to become a national bourgeoisie. The foreign monopolization of the sugar industry obstructed the development of a bourgeois nucleus just as continued reliance on foreign credit inhibited the emergence of an indigenous merchant class. The Dominican-American Convention limited the foreign merchants to a subordinate status in the import-export trade, and local creole merchants were alienated from the higher echelons of commercial activities.

Politics was the only road left open if local political elites were to acquire an economic basis. The state was the "property" that the various factions of the elites sought to control. The Dominican-American Convention, however, limited any control that these elites could have over a bankrupt state. Thus, the crises of Heureaux's dictatorship and Cáceres's regime were in part due to the contradictory integration of the Dominican state into the international capitalist system and the socioeconomic weakness of the local dominant blocs.

5

State Formation and the U.S. Military Occupation

The U.S. military government in the Dominican Republic completed the groundwork for a modern state that served U.S. interests in the Caribbean Basin. The U.S. expansion into the Caribbean was linked to internal struggles in the Dominican Republic leading up to the military occupation of 1916. Dominican nationalist resistance and internal U.S. opposition to the military occupation eventually forced the Wilson administration to incorporate some of the local elite as it organized a new state and prepared to withdraw.

The United States and the Caribbean

U.S. expansion into the Caribbean Basin was fueled by a foreign policy that considered the region a "sphere of influence," by the growing monopolization of the U.S. economy, which led to the export of capital, and by rivalry among Britain, France, Germany, and Italy. By the 1890s the United States had become convinced that these world powers threatened its economic, political, and military security. As early as 1823 the United States had proclaimed the Monroe Doctrine, establishing that any European country's attempt to extend its influence in the Western Hemisphere would be considered a threat to the security of the United States (Gil, 1975:62).

By 1848 the United States had successfully conquered nearly half of Mexico's territory, and some U.S. leaders wanted to expand into Central America. The British, however, were already established on the Caribbean coast of Nic-

Parts of this chapter appeared in "The Formation of the Dominican Capitalist State and the United States Military Occupation of 1916–1924," *Middle Atlantic Council of Latin American Studies, Latin American Essays,* Vol. 4 (1990).

aragua, and U.S. internal political conflicts militated against a war with the British. In 1850 the United States signed the Clayton-Bulwer Treaty, affirming its respect for the territorial integrity of the Central American republics (Guerra Sánchez, 1964:243). Again, in the midst of the Civil War, the United States was unable to keep French troops from occupying Mexico or to prevent Spain from annexing the Dominican Republic. It was not until the beginning of the twentieth century, when the United States emerged as the world's leading economic power, that it was in a position to enforce the Monroe Doctrine. The Spanish-American War offered the opportunity to take direct control of the Philippine Islands and Puerto Rico and to intervene in Cuba. The only major power that could challenge the United States in the Caribbean was Great Britain, which acknowledged U.S. hegemony there by signing the Hay-Paunceforte Treaty in November 1901.

The United States was now the dominant power in the region. On 6 December 1904 President Theodore Roosevelt announced a formula that would terminate all European excuses to intervene in the New World:

> If a nation shows that it knows how to act with a reasonable decency and efficacy in social and political matters, if it keeps order and pays its obligations, then it need fear no interference from the United States. A chronic state of injustice, or an impotence which results in a general loosening of the ties of civilized society, in America or elsewhere, may finally require intervention by some civilized nation, and in the Western Hemisphere the adherence of the United States to the Monroe Doctrine may oblige the United States, though unwillingly, to act in cases of notorious injustice or impotence, as an international power. ... It is just a simple truth to say that every nation, in America or elsewhere, that wishes to keep its freedom, its independence, should understand that, in the last instance, the right of said independence cannot be separated from the responsibility of making a good use of it. (Gil, 1975:70)

The implications of Roosevelt's amendment to the Monroe Doctrine for the small republics of the Caribbean and Central America are evident. None of these republics behaved in the manner Roosevelt prescribed, and therefore all were potential candidates for direct U.S. intervention. Historically, "dollar diplomacy" is associated with President William Howard Taft, but it was Roosevelt who initiated the policy that promoted U.S. financial and banking interests in the region. During the Taft administration the U.S. government promoted private loans in an effort to eliminate European financial activity in the region. When Taft and Secretary of State Philander C. Knox ceased to direct the foreign policy of the United States, this policy was continued by President Woodrow Wilson and his first secretary of state, William Jennings Bryan. Pursued less assiduously during the isolationist 1920s, it was revived in the late 1930s by President Franklin D. Roosevelt and Secretary of State Cordell Hull (Rippy, 1940:138; Callcott, 1977:258–308).

Dollar diplomacy was promoted as a way of fostering democracy and political stability, but in reality it established financial protectorates over several republics in the Caribbean and Central America. This control was closely linked to military interventions, which often occurred when local elites opposed U.S. policy in any way. Soon the United States found itself structuring the local states so that they could respond to its own economic, political, and military concerns in the region. U.S. interventions in Cuba (1898), Panama (1903), Nicaragua (1909), Haiti (1915), and the Dominican Republic (1916) were the main testing grounds for these plans.

Structuring the Modern State

After Cáceres's assassination in 1911, the implementation of the Dominican-American Convention became problematic because of the political instability that ensued. Alfredo Victoria, who at the age of twenty-three had been given the job of reforming the army, emerged as the leading strongman. Because he was too young to occupy the presidency, his uncle, Eladio Victoria, was appointed executive, but the power remained his. Although the Victoria administration received political and financial support from the customs receivership, it could not muster enough power to defeat the opposition headed by Vásquez, Jiménes, and Arias (Letter from W. E. Pulliam, 19 September 1912). In 1912 President Taft sent a commission to mediate between the government and the opposition. Accompanied by seven hundred marines, the commission arrived in Santo Domingo and immediately threatened to occupy the country militarily if the opposition rejected its mediation. The commission soon realized, however, that the Victorias were unpopular and agreed to a compromise candidate, Monsignor Adolfo Nouel (Letter from General McIntyre, 13 October 1912). Nouel took office on 30 November 1912 but abdicated four months later when both Arias and Vásquez demanded positions in the government for their followers. Congress then chose José Bordas Valdez as president.

Still within the framework of the Dominican-American Convention, Bordas received authorization from the United States for a US$1.5 million loan that relieved the government's financial crisis. Nonetheless, he soon faced opposition from within the ranks for taking the administration of the Puerto Plata-Santiago railroad away from Vásquez's party and appointing Arias delegate of the government for the Cibao. The United States offered to supervise the election of a new president, but despite this, the elections proved fraudulent and Bordas was reelected on 5 June 1914. Again, the opposition forced Bordas to resign and agreed on Ramón Báez as provisional president. Báez took office in August 1914 and formed a government with his friends and members of the Jiménes faction. Three important parties participated in the subsequent general elections: Horacistas, Jimenistas and

Velazquistas. With the support of the Velazquistas, Jiménes won and took office in December 1914.

Despite the willingness of local political elites to work with the United States in organizing a strong government, the U.S. State Department excluded them from the process of state formation. The implementation of the Dominican-American Convention had excluded members of Cáceres's own party from receiving political payoffs. Cáceres had had to use force to introduce reforms that adversely affected local business groups while favoring foreign capital. This fact was acknowledged by a U.S. minister to Santo Domingo, William Russell, in a memorandum to the State Department on 15 November 1915: "The Convention of 1907 never could have been secured had it not been for the forceful hand of President Cáceres, who inspired the opposition with abject terror" (Memorandum from William Russell to Frank Polk, 15 November 1915). The leaders who took power after his assassination were for the most part not strong enough to subdue their opponents and were forced to accept greater participation by the United States in organizing the state.

As president, Jiménes supported amendments giving more control of the country's finances and its army and police to the United States. In a letter to Wilson dated 19 October 1915, he acknowledged that the Convention of 1907 had to be modified but recommended postponing any amendments because the republic had just gone through "the painful spectacle of an unjustified civil war. ... The people are very excited and any new pretext for a hideous fratricidal war should be avoided." Jiménes concluded by saying that "once peace is secured in the country, my humble efforts and your noble and sincere aid will drive the moral and material progress of the Dominican Republic" (Letter from President Juan Isidro Jiménes to President Wilson, 19 October 1915).

The United States urged the appointment of U.S. citizens to direct the country's finances and constabulary. The Bordas administration had proposed a post of financial expert, but it was not ratified by Congress. The following description of the financial expert's duties points up the failure of the 1907 Convention and the need for further controls over Dominican finance:

> He was supposed to observe the implementation of the 1907 Convention; formulate a system of public accounting; investigate the means to increase public income and to reduce public spending; verify the validity of any claim against the Dominican government; sign government checks; guide the Dominican government to determine its debts; exercise the power of a customs inspector and director of the department of public works and accountant for all public offices; mediate any conflict between the government and the Customs Receivership, Treasury, and Commerce Departments; aid Dominican officials in preparing their budgets. Finally, to provide a veil of legality this powerful figure's appoint-

ment was made according to the first article of the Convention. (Henríquez Ureña, 1919:62–63)

Jiménes, unable to offer these duties to a foreigner, sent the proposal to Congress for consideration. Arias, now chief of the armed forces, controlled a majority in Congress and opposed the U.S. plan. In the midst of the crisis, Russell offered military aid to Jiménes and was rejected. On 16 May 1916, having had no response to an ultimatum delivered to Arias's forces, the United States proceeded to occupy the city of Santo Domingo.

While the U.S. Marines occupied the country, Arias and his troops left the capital for the northern Cibao, and Congress prepared to discuss the election of a new president. Russell insisted on his own conditions for recognition of the new president, and on learning of Russell's manipulation of the vote, Federico Henríquez y Carvajal withdrew his candidacy. In a last-minute decision, Congress surprised the United States by electing Federico's brother, Francisco, who returned from Cuba to take office on 31 July 1916. In spite of impressive credentials that included medical degrees from Paris and Havana, as well as a law degree and extensive diplomatic experience, Francisco was judged "not satisfactory" by Russell because he had not accepted the U.S. demands. On 15 June, Russell had ordered the customs receivership to assume control over the country's internal finances. In August the receivership cut off funds to the government until it agreed to meet all of the U.S. demands. With the country under military occupation, Henríquez y Carvajal agreed to permit the United States to control not only its finances but also a constabulary. He considered it constitutionally impossible, however, to accede to demands that would give a foreign country plenary power over the republic's government (Munro, 1964:311; Mejía, 1976:113–114; Hoepelman y Senior, 1973: 330–371). With the United States demanding total capitulation, local political elites were entirely excluded from government, and U.S. officials prepared to rule "in the name of the Dominican people."

The Establishment of the U.S. Military Government

The proclamation of a military government on 29 November followed six months of unsuccessful efforts by the U.S. State Department to work out an arrangement similar to that in Haiti, where the previous year the United States had intervened militarily to establish a government in collaboration with certain sectors of the local elite (Schmidt, 1971:82–107; Munro, 1964: 302; Castor, 1971). Obviously, there was a contradiction between that action and Wilson's 1913 announcement that "we are the friends of constitutional government in America; we are more than friends, we are its champions" (Munro, 1964:271). The Wilson administration sought justification by claiming that the Dominican Republic had violated the Convention of 1907 by supposedly increasing the country's public debt: "This military occupation is undertaken with no immediate or ulterior object of destroying the sovereignty of the Republic of Santo Domingo, but on the contrary, is designed to give to that country in returning to a condition of internal order that will enable it to observe the terms of the treaty" (*Proclamation of Occupation and Military Government*, 1925:246–247). Dominican administrators were to remain in office as necessary "under the oversight and control of the United States Forces exercising Military government." Dominican law was to continue in effect as long as it did not conflict with military tribunals. All revenues of the republic were to be collected by the receivership and paid to the military government. "The Forces of the United States in Occupation" were to conduct themselves "in accordance with military law." In effect, a dictatorship had been established.

The Henríquez y Carvajal administration and Congress dissolved themselves in protest. Only the judiciary remained in operation. In place of the Dominican government the U.S. Marines installed a new administration and military.

> At the head of both was the military governor, a powerful figure responsible only to the U.S. Secretary of the Navy. At the top of the military structure was the commander of the Second Provisional Brigade. ... Under the brigade commander were two (later three) regimental commanders, each responsible for a large section of the country. Reporting to them were the commanding officers of the battalions and companies located in the various towns and villages of the republic. Other important officials were the provost marshals. Operating in conjunction with the provost courts, they were the top police and judicial officials of the military government. (Calder, 1984:25)

Captain Harry S. Knapp, the first military governor, filled the various government departments with officers of the U.S. Marines and proceeded to resume a series of measures that Cáceres had initiated, the most important of which were those that created a public works program, a strong national constabulary, a land registration code, and a new tariff.

The Public Works Program

The stated objective of the public works program was to bolster the basic infrastructure of Dominican society. The projects also had significant implications for state formation. In a detailed account presented in early 1917, the military government proposed to construct bridges and roads, repair railroads, and conduct an audit in response to Dominican complaints about the payment of high salaries to incompetent U.S. officials (*Quarterly Report of the Military Government of Santo Domingo*, 1930: 714–716). The following January, the military government unveiled plans to establish a national road network that included a highway from Santo Domingo through the Cibao, La Vega, Moca, and Santiago to Esperanza and Monte Cristi. Two other secondary roads were planned: one running eastward, connecting Seybo Province with Santo Domingo via San Pedro de Macorís, and another westward, connecting Comendador at the Haitian border with San Juan de la Maguana, Azua, Baní, and Santo Domingo (see Map 2.1). The commercial, political, and military importance of this road network was recognized by Military Governor Knapp on 18 October 1918 when he wrote to Secretary of the Navy Josephus Daniels, stating that "it will open up large sections of fertile country, and provide an artery of communication that will be invaluable in both a civic and military way" (*Quarterly Report of the Military Government of Santo Domingo*, 1930:365). Thomas Snowden, Knapp's successor, shared this opinion and wrote:

> It is believed that banditry [guerrilla warfare] could not survive the opening up of the country, which is done as rapidly as funds and the supply of labor will allow; the building of roads through the heart of the country facilitates the opening of new farms and at the same time facilitates military operations against the bandits and this last fact is being allowed for in the inauguration of new roads. (Letter dated August 28, 1919, from the Military Governor, 1934:128)

Opening up farms, developing trade, and establishing military control of the country were essential goals of the military government. These goals were presented as a means of "civilizing" the Dominican people, when in fact they were instruments for organizing a political power responsive to the needs of international capital accumulation. The military government, as Heureaux and Cáceres had, used these new means of communication to exercise political domination over the whole society and to structure a state subordinated to U.S. interests in the Caribbean Basin.

The Constabulary

The constabulary bolstered the unity of the Dominican state and provided the institutional means to exercise a monopoly of power over society. The U.S. plans for a constabulary followed up the strategy of Cáceres by stripping governors of their military power and largely replacing them with U.S. officers (Goldwert, 1962:7). On 17 April 1917 the military government appropriated US$500,000 for organizing, equipping, training, and maintaining a "Dominican constabulary guard" to replace the army, the navy, and the republican guard. Officers of the U.S. marines would be appointed to organize the constabulary until Dominicans were sufficiently well-trained to assume these functions. Members of the disbanded Dominican armed forces would be welcomed into the constabulary provided that they had the necessary qualifications and a clean record (Vega y Pagán, 1956:149–150).

The military governor soon found that Dominicans with any degree of qualification did not want to be associated with the forces of occupation. Volunteers for the constabulary came from the poor, illiterate strata of Dominican society. Harry A. Franck, a U.S. citizen traveling in the country in 1919, heard from a priest that the constabulary "included some of the worst rascals, thieves, and assassins in the country, men far worse than the *gavilleros* [guerrillas], and these often egged the naive Americans on to vent their own private hates" (Franck, 1920:235; Castro García, 1978; Ducoudray, 1976).

Although the development of the constabulary was considered "one of the most important matters to be taken up by the military government," the dreadful state of the new force came to light in 1919 when the U.S. State Department began to examine its achievements in the Dominican Republic. "It was in no way prepared to take over from the marines should a United States civilian government or a withdrawal be instituted" (Calder, 1984:58). It was not until early 1922 that a plan to organize the constabulary began to be developed. U.S. Brigadier General Harry Lee, appointed to accomplish this goal, set out to organize, enlarge, train, and Dominicanize the officer corps and began to restructure the institutional basis of the constabulary, recently renamed the Dominican National Police. By the time the marines withdrew from the country in 1924, they had organized a public coercive force, with a monopoly of power over all of Dominican society. No one except the constabulary had firearms, and improvements in telecommunications and roads allowed it to move rapidly to any place in the country (Calder, 1984:59–62; Welles, 1928:810–817).

The constabulary gave the country a sense of real political unity by destroying the power of traditional regional caudillos. It provided the institutional organization for the emergence of a national military elite that would eventually control national political life because traditional political elites were structurally weak and regionally divided. By bolstering the constabulary, the military government strengthened the coercive apparatus of the state and, perhaps unwittingly, prepared the conditions for the development of dictatorship rather than democracy.

The New Tariff

The policies of the military government were designed not to strengthen the local nonsugar economy but to help a fraction of the import merchants. The tariff of 1920 further weakened the local bourgeoisie. The military government again built on previous efforts to regulate foreign trade and facilitate the entry of agricultural machinery. The Dominican government had been interested in a treaty of reciprocity with the United States, and the military government urged such a treaty. The new tariff reduced duties on over 700 items and put nearly 250 on the duty-free list. This list included transportation equipment, agricultural and machine tools, and industrial machinery, thus stimulating development of the relatively mechanized sugar industry. Duties were reduced on products such as coffee, cacao, and meat (Calder, 1984:75–77; Lozano, 1976:194–198; Muto, 1976:92–101; Del Castillo and Cordero, 1982:115–116).

Favoring the sugar corporations, the 1920 tariff placed the traditional export sectors at a disadvantage by allowing foreign products to enter the country duty-free. Importation of Brazilian coffee accelerated under the new market conditions. Foods traditionally produced in the country began to be replaced by imports. Imported luxury articles often sold at lower prices than indigenous ones, and these new articles created new wants and consequently, new markets. As the import sector grew, small artisanry, unable to compete with the products of U.S. industry, declined. For example, although the incipient shoe industry could in theory import machinery tax-free, it was impossible for local shoemakers to compete with U.S. companies, given the differences in the level of development of the two industries.

The increase in imports as a result of the 1920 tariff unquestionably helped the largest foreign merchants, who imported consumer goods and foodstuffs and "acted both as retailers through large urban stores and as wholesalers to smaller business and vendors," and "a continuing flow of individual immigrants kept the upper level of Dominican commerce in foreign hands"(Muto, 1976:102). Foreign merchants and the itinerant Lebanese and Syrian retailers were integrated into a new structure of dependency generated by the relationship between the importers and their U.S., German, British, and Spanish suppliers. Although largely subordinated to the United States, import merchants benefited marginally from the new arrangements. Producers of traditional agricultural exports (cacao, coffee, and tobacco, for example) and small-scale manufacturers of consumer products suffered from the new competition. In sum, the military government continued the policies implemented during the Cáceres administration, which facilitated foreign investment while discriminating against local business groups.

Local Response to the Military Government

Although the traditional political elites had always wanted to collaborate with the United States, they were initially excluded from the political process by the U.S. occupying forces, which perceived that a strong government could be organized without local cooperation. In 1919 the U.S. State Department reexamined the Dominican political situation and began to revise this policy. Difficulties in organizing a constabulary that could put an end to guerrilla warfare in the east were one reason for this, and nationalist resistance at home and abroad, combined with an effective opposition in the United States, caused Wilson to revise his approach.

Whereas peasants in the north initially offered resistance to the occupying forces, only those of the east formed guerrilla bands to fight the invaders over a long period. These guerrillas were disparagingly referred to as bandits, but the support they received from the population and the fact that it took the marines six years to defeat them clearly show that they were not common criminals. In the most thorough study on the topic to date, Bruce Calder indicates that they

> resented the changes in their lives which resulted from the loss of their land to the large corporations; they resented being unemployed and poor; and they resented the fear and insecurity brought into their daily existence by the aggressive and arbitrary acts of the occupying marines. Some guerrillas, moreover, were conscious that these issues were important to their struggle. They would, for instance, recruit followers by informing peasant smallholders that the North American corporations were planning to take over their land. Going one step further, various guerrilla leaders and groups openly identified themselves as political revolutionaries and claimed regional or national goals. They also conducted themselves, on some occasions, as an irregular government, exacting taxes, enforcing popular law, and dispensing justice. (Calder, 1984:121)

When an end to the guerrilla war was negotiated in 1922, the military government recognized that many rebels had lost their lands and asked the sugar companies to give the peasants "permanent jobs" and subsistence plots. This request seems ironic given that laws enacted during the occupation had sanctioned such dispossessions. Although the guerrilla movement lasted for six years, it was essentially regional and never established any links with the nationalist resistance. The nationalists were urban-based petit-bourgeois and middle-class elements that had been excluded from government largesse since the time of Cáceres, and the military government continued to exclude them.

The nationalist campaign for the withdrawal of the marines was begun by Henríquez y Carvajal immediately after his government was overthrown. In December 1916 he visited the United States to persuade the State Department to change its policy. Unable to do so, he proceeded to organize the Dominican Nationalist Commission, whose objectives were to maintain a constant protest in the United States, Latin America, and Europe; preserve Dominican unity; create a directorate to guide the resistance; and establish a network of nationalist committees in the Dominican Republic to sustain the movement (Calder, 1984:183–184).

Havana became the main center for coordinating nationalist efforts. The campaign was initially successful because it had the support of the Cuban press as well as prominent intellectuals. However, by April 1917, U.S. attention had turned to the war in Europe, and the campaign came to a halt. Meanwhile, Dominicans at home were divided about how to react to the occupation: some groups favored armed resistance while others considered that course to be political suicide. As the end of World War I approached, Dominican nationalists residing in Cuba began to collect money to send president Henríquez y Carvajal to the Versailles Peace Conference. At Versailles he was prevented from meeting the U.S. delegates and was told to present his case to the U.S. State Department in Washington. His subsequent mission to Washington was also unsuccessful; there seemed to be no hope of forcing the United States to end the occupation. Eventually, however, the forceful nationalist resistance to the occupation, coupled with an international campaign of protest and Republican opposition to Wilson's interventionist policy in small countries, led the State Department to begin a series of conversations with Henríquez y Carvajal. On 14 April 1919 he submitted a memorandum in which he restated that the United States had no legitimate reason to continue to occupy the country and rejected the U.S. interpretation of the Convention of 1907:

> The Dominican Government has always understood that the obligation imposed on it was that of contracting no new public debt of the same kind as that guaranteed by the Convention, without previous agreement with the American Government; that a debt arising from a deficit in estimates, by reason of necessary and unusual expenses of war, as well as those due to unforeseen public calamities or to a diminution of income occasioned by bad crops or by fluctuations in merchandise, a debt irregular in its origins, involuntary and impossible to foresee and upon which it is impossible to count, is surely not the debt provided for in the third clause [of the convention of 1907]. (Memorandum from Dr. Henríquez y Carvajal, 1934:109–110)

Despite his disagreements with the United States regarding the convention, President Henríquez y Carvajal was willing to work with the State Department to initiate a gradual process of organizing the country politically and administratively following a broad plan of legal reforms.

The State Department's unwillingness to deal with Dominican affairs began to change when World War I ended and the U.S. Congress refused to ratify the Versailles Treaty. U.S. participation in the war in Europe had caused a noninterventionist backlash at home (Tulchin, 1971:62), and opposition to Wilson's policy in the Caribbean and Central America grew. Articles appeared regularly in the *Nation,* the *New York Times, Current History,* and elsewhere. However, this new attitude should not be interpreted as a break from earlier Latin American policy. Wilson's successors simply reformulated his policy to protect U.S. hegemony.

In the context of the growing isolationist policy of the United States, Dominican nationalists stepped up their campaign for the withdrawal of the military government. Cuba was once more the center of efforts to promote Latin American solidarity. The jurist Emilio Roig de Leuchenring made a galvanizing speech at the Sociedad Cubana de Derecho Internacional that was sent by cable to Latin America and the United States and attracted considerable attention. Sumner Welles wrote:

> the continued Occupation of the Dominican Republic was giving rise to increasing apprehension among the Republics of Latin America. Protests both informal and official, emanating from Latin American Governments, prominent publicists in South America, and from associations throughout the continent, were being addressed continually through the summer and autumn of 1919 to President Wilson, urging the termination of the Occupation and the reestablishment of a Dominican Government. (Welles, 1928:823)

International pressure on Washington was undoubtedly important in turning the State Department's attention to Dominican internal affairs. This political pressure, coupled with the nationalist resistance, led to the easing of repressive policies by the military government, which had imposed "censorship, severe limitations on political activities, and the force represented by armed marines, the provost courts, and the military government's network of spies" (Calder, 1984:189).

In November 1919 the U.S. State Department decided to act on Dominican political affairs without consulting Henríquez y Carvajal's Dominican Nationalist Committee. Governor Thomas Snowden appointed an advisory commission of influential Dominicans including Adolfo Nouel (archbishop of Santo Domingo), Jacinto de Castro, Francisco J. Peynado, and Federico Velázquez. This group was representative of the traditional elites excluded from government politics since the occupation but supportive of the military government. The commission recommended the abolition of press censorship and the provost courts and the initiation of a gradual withdrawal of the marines from the country. In December 1919 it submitted an additional memorandum requesting the military government not to contract on behalf of the republic the new foreign loan of US$5 million that it was seeking. (The occupation was funded not by "foreign aid" or U.S. dollars but by new debt).

The appointment of the advisory commission appeared to signal a shift in the U.S. policy of excluding local elites from the political process. However, contrary to the wishes of the State Department, on 22 December 1919 the military government instituted new censorship, restricting even more severely than in the past the right of free speech and the rights of the press (Calder, 1984:191–193). Having been rejected by the military government and under pressure from the nationalists, the commission resigned in January 1920. Conflict between the military government and the State Department over Dominican affairs became increasingly evident. According to Welles,

> For a period of two years [because of World War I], the Department of State had apparently withdrawn from all supervision over the conduct of affairs in the Dominican Republic. The Navy Department, in view of this, permitted the Military Government to acquire an increasingly large measure of authority in determining

Dominican problems. ... the Military Governor had ... grown to feel that his powers were absolute (Welles, 1928:827)

This conflict helped to mobilize the nationalists. In February 1920 Américo Lugo, a lawyer, and Fabio Fiallo, a poet, founded the Unión Nacional Dominicana (Dominican National Union) to provide "the immediate reestablishment of the republic as an absolutely sovereign state and a prohibition against any collaboration with the military government which might limit Dominican sovereignty after United States withdrawal"(Calder, 1984: 194).

The Union moved quickly to organize nationalist committees in the nation's principal cities and towns. The elite's traditional social clubs became nationalist meeting places. Some clubs ceased inviting the military authorities to their festivities. The Union's first major protest against military rule was the Patriotic Week held from 12–19 May 1920, the main objective of which was to raise consciousness about the military occupation and to generate funds to subsidize the nationalist missions of Henríquez y Carvajal and other leaders. The military government responded with severe repression: "The authorities jailed more than twenty publishers, journalists, poets, and other intellectuals, many of them connected with the republic's most important families" (Calder, 1984:197). Among them were Fiallo and Lugo, who had challenged the authority of the provost courts, and Horacio Blanco Fambona, a Venezuelan journalist who had published a photograph of a peasant victim of marine brutality. The Union sent diplomatic envoys to Latin America and the United States to denounce the repression. Protests again began to reach the State Department from both Latin America and the United States. Once more the United States was forced to reexamine its involvement in the Dominican Republic.

Legitimation and the Withdrawal of the Marines

By brute force, the U.S. Marines had succeeded in laying the material foundations for a strong government in the Dominican Republic, but this was not enough to constitute a legal government minimally acceptable to the majority of the politically active population. Aware of this reality and responding to mounting political pressure in the Dominican Republic, Wilson issued a plan on 23 December 1920 for the gradual withdrawal of the marines. The plan included the formation of a second advisory commission composed of representative Dominicans, meaning those traditional politicians who had been advising the military government informally. A technical adviser was included to help revise the constitution and draft a new electoral law (Welles, 1928:830–831). The Union condemned any form of collaboration with the military government and proposed its own formula for withdrawal with no strings attached—a plan unacceptable to the United States. The rejection of the U.S. plan by the nationalists intimidated the conservative faction of the local elites, who were charged with "treason to the homeland" for their collaboration. Even so, the United States persisted in including this faction in the political process.

When he assumed office in 1921, U.S. President Warren G. Harding found himself faced with the problem of how to withdraw the marines. He had attacked Wilson's policies and the occupation during his campaign, and he and Secretary of State Charles Evans Hughes were reportedly determined to end the U.S. military presence in the Dominican Republic. "They believed that abandoning armed intervention in favor of advice and counsel would foster good will in Latin America and ultimately benefit the United States by enabling it to garner the trade and support of the region" (Grieb, 1969:425). Although this approach seemed to offer a unique opportunity to improve Caribbean relations, its translation into practice in the Dominican case produced results not significantly different from those of previous policies. The United States was still committed to legitimating the activities of the military government, thereby making the new state structurally subordinated to U.S. interests.

On 14 June 1921 the Harding administration issued a second proclamation regarding the withdrawal of the military government. This plan, built on the earlier Wilson plan, called for the ratification of all the acts of the military government, the validation of a US$2.5 million loan to complete public works in progress, an extension of the duties of the general receiver of Dominican customs, the maintenance of a constabulary organized and directed by U.S. officers appointed by the Dominican president upon the designation of the U.S. president, and the organization of elections under U.S. tutelage (Welles, 1928:843–844).

In response to the Harding plan, the Dominican National Union called for a demonstration in front of the governor's office, and over three thousand people gathered there. The protest surprised the military government and officials in Washington, and the obvious strength of the nationalist movement led Henríquez y Carvajal to take a more confrontational stance toward the United States. It also allowed nationalists to exert more pressure on the local conservative groups that appeared to be working behind the scenes to reach a pact with the United States. Lugo warned nationalists against the traitors who were willing to collaborate with the military government: "The military occupation cannot be considered as anything but a force majeure; the victim of it is not obliged to do anything. ... once we accept a change we will have ceased to be victims of a force majeure ... by granting an entitlement that legitimizes an injustice (Jaime Julia, 1976:29).

As a lawyer, Lugo understood that behind the U.S. plan for withdrawal was the need to legitimize the actions of the military government. The United

States needed a local group willing to accept the intervention as legal, and therefore it sought to induce the leading members of the traditional political parties to come to terms with it. Yet the nationwide popularity of the Union forced the conservatives to move cautiously. Samuel Robinson, Snowden's successor, issued a clarification that tempered the original proclamation, and moderates within the nationalist faction urged Henríquez y Carvajal to accept the plan. Nonetheless, nationalists remained more or less united and continued to voice their now standard objections to U.S. control of elections, the Dominican military, internal revenues, and the process of amending the constitution (Calder, 1984:211).

On 7 December 1921 nationalists met with traditional politicians in Puerto Plata and signed a nine-point pact designed to effect the withdrawal of the marines. The principal points of the Harding plan were dismissed, various constitutional and administrative reforms were recommended, and the diplomatic mission of the advisory commission was endorsed (Hoepelman y Senior, 1973:312–316). Because of inherent political differences between the parties, the Puerto Plata pact was not, however, translated into meaningful political action, and the two sides reached an impasse. The U.S. State Department took advantage of the situation to announce that because the Dominican people were unwilling to cooperate in the implementation of the Harding plan, the process of withdrawal would be postponed "until such time as the urgent public works, now in process of construction, have been completed, and an adequate Dominican constabulary is functioning" (Letter dated February 10, 1922, from the Secretary of State, 1938:10–11).

The Hughes-Peynado Agreement

By this time the funds raised during the Patriotic Week were exhausted, and Henríquez y Carvajal was dispirited and plagued by personal problems. Hopes that the Harding administration would accept a compromise favorable to the Dominican cause withered away. With the Dominican National Union in disarray, traditional political leaders were now able to step in with their compromise solutions. In this context, Francisco Peynado traveled to Washington to discuss a way to break the impasse created by the intransigence of the nationalists. Peynado was used to working with the United States. He had been a lawyer for sugar companies, a Dominican minister to Washington, and the head of a public safety committee established to maintain order in the early days of the military invasion and was thus well equipped to work out a solution with the State Department. He was prepared to compromise on key issues, including the validation of the executive orders of the military government, which legalized the landownership of the sugar companies, reformed public administration, regulated the forces of public order, and guaranteed the loans incurred by the military government on behalf of the occupied republic. In addition, he offered a new idea that seemed to satisfy Washington and the traditional political leaders: the creation of a provisional government. The main function of the provisional government was to preside over the transition from U.S. military rule to a new civilian government by conducting general elections to choose a Dominican congress. Once elected, Congress was to validate all the important actions of the military government. Peynado suggested that before these negotiations could be concluded it would be necessary to obtain the support of the country's main political leaders. Although pro-U.S. leaders such as Federico Velázquez, Horacio Vásquez, and Elías Brache were invited to discuss the future of the Dominican state with the United States, Henríquez y Carvajal, Lugo, Fiallo, and other prominent nationalists were not.

The plan was made public in September 1922. Named for Peynado and Secretary of State Hughes, it proposed a provisional government to be elected by the members of a U.S.-appointed commission composed of Vásquez, Velázquez, Brache, Peynado, and Nouel. The provisional government was to organize presidential elections and elections for a new congress. The newly formed Dominican government would then recognize the validity of all the executive orders issued by the military government as well as the bond issue of 1918 and the twenty-year, 5.5 percent customs administration bond issue authorized in 1922. The tariff of 1920 would be retained, and the Convention of 1907 would remain in force and referred to the Dominican Congress for its approval (Welles, 1928:866–871).

In sum, these initial agreements meant that for the first time since the intervention the United States had struck a deal that would give the new state a semblance of legality—something that Lugo, Henríquez y Carvajal, Fiallo, and others had resisted. Nationalists quickly launched a campaign denouncing the agreement and charging that the U.S. military occupation of the country was illegal. Again, Lugo proposed a total withdrawal with no strings attached (Jaime Julia, 1976:41–48). Nonetheless, the agreement with the traditional political parties had critically wounded the nationalists.

The U.S.-engineered Commission of Representatives elected Juan Bautista Vicini Burgos to head the provisional government. During his term in office from 1922 to 1924, Vicini Burgos worked closely with Sumner Welles, Harding's special commissioner. Welles traveled all over the country with representatives of the conservative political factions, attempting to explain and gain support for the Hughes-Peynado agreement. In fact, Welles had helped frame the agreement and worked behind the scenes to direct the commission and the provisional government (Ortega Frier, 1973). He advised the provisional government on preparing for general elections and pressed the military government to complete unfinished public works projects and to speed up the training and organization of the constabulary. General elections were held on 15 March 1924, and Vásquez won by an overwhelming majority. Congress had already been elected and was soon convened to legitimize the actions of the military government. Once these important tasks were completed, on 12 July the U.S. military forces withdrew.

Conclusion

Difficulties in organizing a strong government favorable to U.S. interests in the Caribbean Basin at first forced the United States to exclude Dominican political elites from the state-building process. Nonetheless, the U.S. military government that was established in 1916 continued earlier efforts to promote public works projects that unified the state and encouraged capitalist development. When the formation of a military organization without the collaboration of local elites proved problematic in the context of widespread nationalist resistance and opposition from the U.S. public, Wilson initiated a process that would integrate a faction of the local political elite into the occupation regime. Dominican nationalists rejected this approach because it included the legitimation of the military government. The traditional conservatives took advantage of the ensuing impasse to negotiate the establishment of a provisional government and the withdrawal of the marines.

Most of the policies of the military government were aimed at strengthening the state's military apparatus and the position of the U.S. sugar and timber corporations. The traditional export economy was crushed by a new tariff that granted duty-free entry to many foreign products. Only the largest import merchants profited, and those, marginally. Creole merchants were further distanced from the higher echelons of the merchant class. Finally, the embryonic local bourgeoisie was structurally weakened by the actions of the government of occupation, and a military elite gradually began to form within the newly equipped and reorganized constabulary. The U.S. military government helped make traditional regional caudillos obsolete, but by fostering a strong military apparatus, it prepared the way for the reemergence of a national military caudillo.

6

Class and State Formation Under Trujillo

The dictatorship of Rafael L. Trujillo represented the most comprehensive of these efforts to create a modern Dominican state, but despite its success the state continued to rest on weak and underdeveloped social structures. This made it impossible for it to survive the collapse of the dictatorship without returning to the status quo ante.

The Historical Context

When the U.S. Marines left the Dominican Republic in 1924, neocolonial ties with the new Dominican state were left firmly in place. The Dominican-American Convention of 1924 legalized actions of the military government, including its new foreign loans, and extended U.S. control of Dominican customs houses. The Dominican government was prevented from increasing its foreign debt without the agreement of the United States. Clearly, the Dominican state was not sufficiently autonomous to intervene in the economy.

The petit bourgeoisie, which had produced a generation of nationalist leaders, had been left out of the new political alliance. The new state was organized as a liberal democratic state with a civilian elite formally in control of political power and in charge of the military elite, which had been trained and equipped by the U.S. military government and was expected to obey the civilian government. These arrangements engendered new difficulties:

First, local groups were in fact politically incapable of managing the state apparatuses because of their marginal roles in the main productive and commercial sectors. Second, the bureaucratic-military elite was structurally incapable of carrying out its economic project and exercising political control, partly because of the institutional framework that assigned them a marginal role and partly because the main economic sector was controlled by foreigners and the marginal sectors by local power groups. (Lozano, 1976:258)

Eight years of military occupation had demonstrated that the United States could not rule the Dominican Republic directly. It had no choice but to enlist the collaboration of local elites to manage internal political affairs. With the exception of the Dominican National Union, the political parties and factions that emerged during the last two years of the military occupation were under the political hegemony of the United States. These political elites had agreed to guarantee the political and administrative conditions that would permit capitalist accumulation in terms that favored foreign investors. In effect, U.S. diplomatic officials were the arbitrators between the different factions of the dominant sectors and at times exercised greater power than the national government. The U.S legation was both judge and party to the trial.

The structural weakness of the traditional elites and Trujillo's links to an external power created the historical circumstances for the emergence of a military caudillo of a new type. Unlike a traditional regional caudillo, backed by armed civilians, the new caudillo was supported by a relatively well-trained and well-equipped constabulary with a virtual monopoly of power. The disarming of citizens had effectively destroyed the military capabilities of regional caudillos. At the same time, the weakness of the civilian elites and the emergence of a more cohesive military elite favored the evolution of a national military caudillo. The national character of the state and the strength of its repressive apparatus were essential to the emergence of Rafael L. Trujillo as that caudillo.

After the withdrawal of the marines, conflict developed between the political and military elites over the political power that would provide them with a solid economic base. Horacio Vásquez created the political opportunity for the Dominican army's entry into national politics when he announced his interest in reelection. He had already suffered a loss of popularity when he unilaterally extended the presidential term for two years. Now a new and powerful opposition developed, and the president's Partido Nacional became increasingly divided, with some of its prominent members joining the Partido Progresista of Federico Velázquez, the Partido Liberal of Desiderio Arias, or the Partido Republicano of Rafael Estrella Ureña, a political friend of Trujillo. Trujillo did not publicly support any of these parties, but when Vásquez appeared to be losing political control upon his return from a medical trip to the United States in 1930, it became clear that Trujillo was deeply involved in politics and was already the leader of the Dominican military elite.

Trujillo had been admitted to the constabulary in 1919 as a second lieutenant and had rapidly risen to the upper ranks. He became Vásquez's protégé and as such, by 1930 he became the unquestioned chief of the constabulary, which had been transformed from a police organization into an army. International economic events played a crucial role in his assumption of power. The devastating effects of the great economic depression on the industrialized countries had had repercussions for Latin America, which was economically dependent on them. Thus the Dominican economy was suddenly paralyzed in the midst of a developing political crisis. The various groups opposed to Vásquez's reelection had formed a broad front. Trujillo led Vásquez to believe that he was trustworthy when, in fact, he was plotting to overthrow him. In February 1930 he engineered a simulated military uprising in Santiago with troops reportedly marching on Santo Domingo. Vásquez summoned Trujillo to his office and asked frankly, "Am I still the president?" Trujillo responded that it was so and said that he awaited Vásquez's orders. This was not the case, however. Trujillo countered by replacing army commanders loyal to Vásquez with his allies and allowed the "Santiago rebels" to take Santo Domingo. This situation resulted in a political crisis that forced Vásquez to resign. Trujillo became the de facto ruler of the Dominican Republic (Galíndez, 1984; Franco, 1992).

The Concentration of Power

Conflict between civilian and military elites ended with Trujillo's assumption of power; he destroyed any political opposition and ensured that no future opposition would develop. The development of a strong power structure was one of Trujillo's first tasks. He seemed to understand that certain state structures were necessary to preserve his political power, and to this end he concentrated on the development of the military, the Partido Dominicano, Congress, and the government bureaucracy.

The military became his main instrument of control. Little more than an expanded constabulary in 1930, the Dominican army was rapidly transformed into the most powerful military in the Caribbean Basin. In 1931 the military budget was $1,141,000, slightly more than 11 percent of the national budget. By 1936 it had risen to $1,690,000, or 16 percent of the total annual budget; this increase outstripped a moderate increase in total government revenue (Wiarda, 1970:46). The military budget continued to claim larger and larger shares of the national budget; by 1940 it had reached 21 percent and by 1956–1957, 25 percent. In addition, in 1957 the military spent US$1 million for U.S. military assistance and an undisclosed amount to buy sophisticated weaponry (Ornes, 1958:138). In sum, the budget statistics show a steady increase with or without external threats. The military had become a bastion of political patronage and an instrument of internal coercion.

Although Trujillo turned the Dominican armed forces into a well-equipped, disciplined, and effective force for controlling the citizenry, he always exercised not only full legal authority but also an extralegal, personal control. Like Heureaux, Trujillo supervised the most minute details of the military, including organization, quartering, clothing, equipment, transportation, communications, and other administrative matters. He frequently shuffled its personnel at all levels to ensure that no individual officer or branch would gain too much power. He also packed the armed forces with relatives or officers who were loyal rather than qualified. The most grotesque example of Trujillo's use of the army for political ends was the Haitian massacre. Late in September 1937, Trujillo visited the border city of Dajabón and accused Haitian peasants of stealing Dominican cattle. On 1 and 2 October Dominican troops killed more than twelve thousand Haitian peasants. At first Trujillo denied any government participation in the "incidents" and attempted to cover up the massacre by calling it a "fight" over livestock between Dominican and Haitian peasants.

The Dominican sociologist Luis Fernando Tejada Olivares (1979) has explained the massacre as part of a much larger process of land accumulation by Trujillo and the emerging economic elite. Susy Castor (1983), a Haitian sociologist, has attacked this position for ignoring the deeply rooted racism that permeated the dominant ideology of the Dominican Republic. Both economic and ideological aspects are undoubtedly key elements in explaining the massacre, but the political dimension cannot be overlooked. The dictatorship did not yet control commercial activity in the border regions, and smuggling was commonplace there. Haitian currency circulated as far east as Santiago, and Haitian language and customs were increasingly influencing significant segments of the Dominican population in the west. This pattern of development ran counter to Trujillo's goal of making the Dominican population more homogeneous in his own terms (i.e., Spanish-speaking, Catholic, and, of course, obedient to his authority). In addition, he worried that his opponents might organize against his dictatorship in the poorly regulated border regions. Thus, the state needed to have control over all of the national territory, and the gradual encroachment of Haitians could not be tolerated. From this perspective, the massacre of thousands of Haitian peasants can be seen as part of Trujillo's drive to create a modern national state.

The Haitian government was markedly slow in reacting to the massacre. It took militant protest by the Haitian people before the government sought U.S. mediation to settle the issue. The negotiation process was slow, but eventually Trujillo agreed to pay an indemnity of US$750,000 to the families of the victims—$250,000 in cash, with the rest to be paid over a five-year period. The Haitian government later agreed to accept the reduced sum of US$270,000 (Crassweller, 1966:172–173), most of which went into the pockets of officials.

Although Trujillo had tried to conceal the massacre, the story had leaked out, and he was forced to attempt to polish his image abroad with the assistance of Washington lobbyists. His invitation to Washington in 1939 was a clear signal that the United States still backed him, but despite that support he had to decline to be a candidate in the 1938 elections. He chose Manuel Troncoso de la Concha to run for president in his place. Congress named Trujillo head of the military and gave him power nearly equal to that of the president.

Aware that a leader cannot rule by force alone, Trujillo proceeded to create the Partido Dominicano to "encourage" the Dominican people to accept and support his regime. Robert Crassweller has summarized his role in the party:

> The statutes of the party supported his vehement personalism with remarkable thoroughness. Everything was concentrated in the hands of the Chief. Branches were established in every community and province, but all officials, whether local, provincial, or national, were appointed by Trujillo, and he named all paid employees, authorized all expenses, imposed his ideas for programs, had legal authority to interpret the statutes as he wished, and resolved all matters not set forth in the statutes.
>
> At once the Dominican Party became part of the official government in practice. The Chairman of its Central Committee (Junta Superior Directiva) held the rank of a Minister of State. The expenses of the party and the cost of its programs were met by a flat 10 percent deduction from the paychecks of all members. In the case of members who were public officials, the deductions were withheld by the Treasury. ... The party began to serve as an instrument of social service, as if it were a huge welfare department. (Crassweller, 1966:116)

The party gave free rein to the chief and allowed for the "legal" extraction of riches from its members, practically the nation's entire voting-age population. It was the only party in the country, and no one dared create an opposition party without Trujillo's explicit permission. As a state institution designed to gather the support of all of the nation's social groups and classes, the party carried out civic projects, dispensed medicine, provided meals for the poor, and contributed to agricultural and highway-building programs. All party activities were conducted in the name of Trujillo, and no opportunity was lost to praise and flatter him. In 1935, Mario Fermín Cabral, who had welcomed the U.S. military in 1916, proposed changing the name of the capital from Santo Domingo to Trujillo City. By January 1936 all the legal formalities had been taken care of, and the Dominican Congress had approved the change. Trujillo, of course, feigned reluctance but accepted the honor. In 1936 the Ministry of Foreign Relations nominated him for the Nobel Peace Prize in recognition of the border accords that had been reached with the Haitian government.

An important function of the Partido Dominicano was to secure nationwide support for Trujillo's electoral campaigns. It is worth noting that Trujillo respected the formalities of a liberal democracy; elections were held every four years during his regime. The elections, though, were staged events. When Trujillo was a candidate, he won by a landslide. The party underwrote huge campaign rallies to give him the legitimacy that his regime needed to project it nationally and internationally. The Dominican Republic was a one-party state: there was no disagreement between the Partido Dominicano and the Dominican government.

The military and the Partido Dominicano served as mechanisms for increasing the power of the state. The military was instrumental in establishing state control over the border regions and buttressing political domination nationwide. The Partido Dominicano also sought to strengthen Trujillo's political hegemony, but it used a more persuasive approach.

The government bureaucracy and Congress played key roles in concentrating political power. Despite the virtual absence of economic growth during the 1930s, Trujillo orchestrated the rapid expansion of the government, creating ten new institutions, including the Internal Revenues Agency, the Ministry of Telecommunications, the Ministry of Public Health, the Ministry of Industry and Commerce, a Land Court, and others in the 1930s. During the 1940s he created seven more, including a nationally controlled customs receivership, a government-sponsored credit union, the Reserve Bank, and the Central Bank. The creation of these institutions led to an expansion in government employment as the number of middle-level technical workers and professional administrators went from 5,579 in 1935 to 12,168 in 1950 and to 23,190 in 1960. The bureaucrats functioned with disciplined loyalty to one individual—Trujillo. As he had with the military, he chose bureaucrats for loyalty rather than efficiency, placed his relatives in key positions, and shuffled personnel so that no one would accumulate sufficient power to undermine him.

Far from counterbalancing executive power, Congress also operated along personalist lines, enacting laws and constitutional reforms to strengthen Trujillo's policies and programs. Trujillo maintained such tight control of Congress that Dominican legislators had to sign resignation letters before assuming office. Again, loyalty was the paramount qualification for office. Like all public employees, congressmen had to submit to loyalty checks and provide detailed information about their private and public lives.

The military, the Partido Dominicano, the bureaucracy, and Congress were the main institutional pillars of the dictatorship. They allowed Trujillo to control nearly all national civic institutions. Although Trujillo accumulated substantial personal wealth and capital in the 1930s, he was unable to control the national economy because the nation's purse strings were still held by the United States. The Dominican state functioned within the political scheme created by the 1924 Dominican-American Convention. The U.S. dollar was still Dominican currency, and the Dominican government could not increase its debt without the consent of the U.S. government. Thus, the sovereignty of the Dominican state remained compromised, and this prevented the Trujillo dictatorship from operating with a greater degree of autonomy (Maríñez, 1993:17–37). Trujillo managed to regain control of the custom houses in

1941 and to pay off the external debt in 1947, thus ending the most blatant forms of foreign intrusion in national affairs, but when he was assassinated in 1961 U.S. intrusion resumed with a blend of old and new mechanisms of domination.

State Formation and Foreign Intervention

When Trujillo assumed power in 1930, Dominican debts had not yet surpassed the limits set by the 1924 Convention. Although Vásquez had not paid interest on the external debt from 1927 to 1929, the Dominican government could still borrow foreign money. The necessity to continue paying interest and principal on the debt created a difficult situation for Trujillo because Dominican export-import activity had plummeted as a result of the world recession. Thus, his political survival depended on the United States. He declared a state of emergency and, with tacit U.S. support, asked the Dominican Congress to authorize a moratorium on interest payments that would free funding for government operations and social services. Going beyond the intent of the law, he also bought weapons for the military and implemented politically popular public works projects.

The moratorium of 1931 and its extension in 1932 slowed down capital outflows, allowing the regime to control budget deficits, keep money in circulation, and continue public works projects that provided employment. Despite the increased demand for social services, Trujillo allocated 27 percent of the national budget to the military from 1931 to 1933, and U.S. officials in the Dominican Republic considered this "absolutely necessary to preserve law and order" (Vega, 1990:83). At the same time, the moratorium strengthened Dominican dependence on the United States. In fact, Trujillo not only left the customs receivership to be administered by a U.S.-appointed director but also allowed it to collect internal taxes, thus for the first time granting the U.S. government control of all sources of revenue. The Convention of 1924 had established that U.S. control of customs houses would last only until 1941, but in 1931 Trujillo proposed the issuance of bonds payable in thirty, forty, and one hundred years to stabilize the Dominican economy, and they were issued with U.S. approval. Thus U.S. control of Dominican customs houses would have lasted another one hundred years, because U.S. holders of Dominican bonds counted on U.S. protection under the terms of the convention (Vega, 1990:96).

Improvement in the economy in the 1940s allowed Trujillo to seek autonomy from the United States. In an effort to terminate U.S. control over Dominican finances, he paid his Washington lobbyists handsomely to influence U.S handling of the Dominican external debt. It is worth recalling that U.S. Marines had trained Trujillo during the military occupation of 1916–1924, and he had developed relationships with officers in the marines that would be valuable throughout his dictatorship. When he visited Washington in 1939, the U.S. Army welcomed him with a reception, and his former marine trainers received him warmly (Vega, 1992:227–256). The renewal of these ties helped Trujillo to develop a Washington network that facilitated the negotiation of the Convention of 1940, which put an end to the U.S. control of Dominican customs houses.

By the eve of World War II, the Convention of 1924 had become an anachronism and an obstacle to U.S. security concerns. It could not be terminated until all Dominican foreign debts were paid, but in 1940 the United States was preparing to go to war and could not afford to pay attention to a small group of American and European owners of Dominican bonds. In the event of war, the United States would need Latin American support, and aware of this, Trujillo publicly pointed out that the Convention of 1924 violated the Good Neighbor Policy. Thus, he seized the opportunity to terminate the compromised status of the Dominican state.

The Convention of 1940 is known in the Dominican Republic as the Trujillo-Hull Treaty; Trujillo popularized it that way to signal that the era of foreign-imposed conventions was over. Acting as minister of foreign relations, he signed the convention himself in order to be able to take credit for the restoration of Dominican sovereignty. To replace the U.S.-controlled customs receivership, the convention created a customs office with Dominican citizens appointed to administer it. The Dominican government could now modify its tariff laws without restriction and increase its debt without U.S. consent.

The new political and economic freedom did have its limitations. The new director-general of customs was jointly appointed by the Dominican government and holders of Dominican bonds, most of whom were either U.S. citizens or Europeans. The Dominican government pledged all of its revenue to guarantee the payment of the external debt, and all its revenues were to be deposited in the Dominican branch of the New York–based National City Bank. Moreover, the government was forbidden to withdraw money from the bank without the consent of its bondholders. Like the Convention of 1924, this convention gave the United States most-favored-nation status without reciprocity, requiring the Dominican Republic to grant the United States the same reduction in tariffs that it gave to any other nation (Vega, 1990:433–434). Thus, foreign intervention in Dominican finances had been reduced but not eliminated, because the U.S. government continued to exert a degree of control over the payment of the external debt. Nonetheless, the convention signaled the end of the protectorate status of the Dominican state. It was also a turning point in the process of state formation: the Dominican state could now control the nation's finances and promote the development of a new economic elite with significantly less foreign restriction.

The war drove up the prices of Dominican sugar and other export products on the world market. Sugar showed the most spectacular increase, moving from $1.00 a pound in the 1930s to $2.65 in 1942. As the price of sugar spiraled upward, the Dominican government increased taxes on sugar and other exports. Total government income increased steadily from US$12,149,568 in 1940 to US$29,575,585 in 1945 and to US$43,900,619 in 1946 (Cassá, 1982b:Table No. VI–19). This upsurge in commodity prices enabled Trujillo to pay off the entire foreign debt and terminate the Convention of 1940, but not in the way commonly supposed. He borrowed internally to do so—a fact ignored by Trujillo's propagandists and still unknown to many in the Dominican Republic. Most of the hard currency needed to pay the external debt came from money "lent" to the government by private depositors who owned 72 percent of the money deposited in the Reserve Bank (Vega, 1990:579). These were not "loans" as commonly understood, because Trujillo had used his political power to force private depositors to provide them. The new internal debt was paid off with the revenues provided by higher export taxes on sugar, rice, tobacco, cacao, coffee, and other export products. Trujillo did not discuss these details on 17 July 1947, when he announced the end of foreign control of Dominican finances. A few days later, a check for US$9,271,855.55 was presented to the U.S. official who still oversaw the payment of the foreign debt.

No one in the Dominican Republic opposed an action that ended foreign control of Dominican finances, and Trujillo moved quickly to restructure the newly independent state. In October 1947 Congress approved a series of laws regulating the Dominican banking system, including the Central Bank, the Monetary Board, and the Central Bank's agreement with the Bretton Woods Accord, the defining economic agreement between the postwar Western nations. The Dominican peso was created and quickly replaced the U.S. dollar as the national currency.

International political and economic events helped the Dominican state move from financial protectorate status to full, formal independence. Soon, however, new mechanisms of foreign domination began to develop: the International Monetary Fund (IMF), the World Bank, the Import-Export Bank, and other emerging international institutions that exerted control over the economies of developing countries. Even so, ending U.S. control of Dominican finances was an important qualitative change in the process of state formation. It paved the way for a new stage of dependent capitalist development and an opportunity to consolidate the Dominican state and the Trujillist elite that supported it.

The Formation of a Trujillist Economic Elite

When Trujillo took control of the Dominican government in 1930, he was already a wealthy man, but he was not the representative of a national bourgeoisie. Instead, he led a political movement that consolidated national political institutions and used them to spearhead a process of capital accumulation that provided a solid economic foundation for a new economic elite. The formation of this Trujillist elite began with a process of accumulation directed by the state that expropriated traditional elites and rural and urban producers—in sum, most of the economically active population. First came the large-scale eviction of peasants. By the mid-1930s thousands had lost their lands to the dictator's cattle business near Santo Domingo, and even the Haitian massacre can be seen as part of the process in that their small parcels of land were confiscated. Next, laws were enacted to create a government monopoly on basic consumer goods such as milk, salt, beef, oil, cigarettes, and shoes. Producers of basic foodstuffs had to pay a regressive income tax that applied as well to small businessmen and craftsmen. Having neutralized the competition and secured a monopoly for himself, Trujillo introduced tariff reductions for all export products. Accumulation was also served by the concession of permits to export products; and for products in which the dictator had an economic interest, in addition to acquiring permits, exporters had to pay him separate cash quotas. Another mechanism of accumulation was the buying and selling of state companies. When one of the companies that Trujillo had acquired from the state proved unprofitable, he would sell it back to the state as if it were in perfect financial condition (Gómez, 1979:99–100; Báez, 1978:86–89; Cassá, 1982b:421–450; Tejada Olivares, 1979; Maríñez, 1993:39). Similarly, he used state funds to conduct his personal business operations, and the state provided the necessary infrastructure and funds to ensure the success of those operations.

The new economic elite that benefited from this model of accumulation was both highly concentrated and closely tied to Trujillo's family. Franc Báez suggests how close-knit that elite was:

> Ramón Saviñón Lluberes, Trujillo's brother-in-law, managed the real estate business, the industrial slaughterhouse, and the national lottery; his uncle Teófilo Pina Chevalier was president of San Rafael Insurance; Francisco Martínez Alba, his brother-in-law, managed Read Hardware and exercised control over import permits; Frank Parra, a relative of the Parra Alba family, exercised control over export permits; an American known as Hansard managed the monopoly over salt and the Naviera, a merchant marine company. Late in the 1930s, the Naviera was managed by former Colonel McLaughlin, whose daughter was the girlfriend of Héctor B. Trujillo, Trujillo's brother; María Martínez, Trujillo's wife, operated the army's laundry as well as supplies of medicine, charcoal, and potable water. She also had a monopoly on usury nationwide. Another brother owned much of the real estate of Bonao. (Báez, 1978:91)

This economic elite had extraordinary political and economic power. Trujillo, of course, played the key role. Anselmo Paulino, one of his personal assistants, estimated that in 1954 there were forty to fifty Dominican men who, in property and money, were worth US$250,000–300,000, from ten to twelve who possessed US$300,000–500,000, about ten who possessed US$1 million, and five who had more than that (Bosch, 1984:409). These figures underestimate the wealth of the Trujillist elite, but they do point to their economic power in Dominican society.

The traditional economic elites were unable to expand as rapidly as this new state-backed group, but they certainly held their own and entered the post-Trujillo period with significant amounts of capital. The Vicini family, for example, was never expropriated by Trujillo, and the traditional northern Cibao group, including the Bermúdez, Brugal, Cabral, Tavares, Grullón, and other prominent landowning families remained more or less intact as well.

By the 1940s the Trujillist elite had nearly monopolized the mainstream of the Dominican economy, and under Trujillo's leadership the state had achieved relative autonomy from foreign domination. The Trujillist elite had not yet come into open conflict with the U.S. sugar concerns that had investments in the country because the foreigners paid the higher export tax that Trujillo had demanded. However, the elite's accumulation of capital, the full payment of the foreign debt, and the creation of a central bank ready to lend money to top investors made new investment in internal economic development possible. In addition, high sugar prices throughout the 1940s motivated Trujillo to go into the sugar business, setting the stage for conflict with foreign sugar producers.

It is nearly impossible to establish which companies Trujillo personally bought and which he bought in the name of the state. He started his sugar business with the Catarey sugar mill in Villa Altagracia, near Santo Domingo, and followed up in 1952 with the Central Río Haina. In 1953 this latter operation bought the Central Ozama, and Trujillo bought Amistad, Porvenir, and Santa Fe, the last two being among the largest milling centers in the republic, owned at the time by the South Porto Rico Sugar Company. The South Porto Rico and the West Indies Sugar Company had been the country's main sugar enterprises. Dominican sugar had been marketed in England since the 1920s, and the South Porto Rico and West Indies Sugar had been doing well in that market and elsewhere in Europe. From 1945 to 1952 these two corporations jointly reported net profits of US$85,353,375 (Báez, 1978:95). Undoubtedly it was these profits that prompted Trujillo to enter the business. For years the two companies had had a good working relationship with Trujillo, but now that the dictator was interested in their business, the relationship turned sour. In 1953 Trujillo initiated an assault on the sugar industry, denouncing working conditions in the fields and the *bateyes* (the villages where Haitians and Dominicans cane cutters lived). The South Porto Rico and West Indies Sugar, both owned by U.S. citizens, threatened to complain to the U.S. State Department—without success. Trujillo was able to buy out West Indies Sugar, paying US$35,830,000 for the company's five mills in 1956 (Gómez, 1979:106; Báez, 1978:101).

The Trujillist elite's incursion into the sugar business was accompanied by a drive to industrialize the nation via import substitution. State-led import-substitution industrialization had been introduced in the larger nations of Latin America in the 1920s, and the rise of populist governments in Mexico, Brazil, and Argentina had stimulated the development of such programs in the 1930s and 1940s. The Dominican Republic, however, had no such programs until the 1940s and 1950s, when a solid industrial elite emerged under Trujillo's leadership and protection. The landmarks were the plans for textiles (1945), chemical fertilizers (1945), cement and gypsum (1947), sacks and cord (1949), iron parts, metal, weaponry, beds, and plows (1950), glass (1955), rubber products (1958), curtain rods and agricultural equipment, barbed wire, asbestos, bauxite, and iron beds (1959), and so on (Gómez, 1979). Trujillo's import-substitution industrialization policy was based on a series of incentives and concessions given mostly to the Trujillist elite or to foreign investors. The policy emerged from contracts negotiated with prominent foreign merchants who had resided in the country since the turn of the century. Baduí Dumit, Jesús Armenteros Seisdedos, Francisco Martínez Alba, and José María Bonetti Burgos were among the prominent merchants to invest in industry. Most of these investors became Dominican, and today their descendants are part of the Dominican bourgeoisie. Industrialization policy exempted investors from local taxes and allowed them to import duty-free all the machinery they needed to initiate their industrial activities. In exchange they were to promote import substitution, generate hard currency, create employment, bring new technologies to the country, and, of course, advance national industrial development.

The Trujillo regime embarked on a series of joint ventures with foreign investors that sought to manufacture products unavailable in the international market because of the trade interruption brought about by World War II. These ventures usually received special treatment because Trujillo was involved. For example, Luis I. Pokrass, a U.S. businessman, built an alcohol distillery plant that was projected to replace 40 percent of the gasoline imported nationwide. The Dominican state promised to develop the infrastructure necessary to operate the plant in addition to providing duty-free entry for any machinery necessary and exemption from local taxes. The business failed because oil from the Netherlands Antilles was available without interruption during the war, and Pokrass and Trujillo sold it to a Dominican conglomerate comprised of Casa Bermúdez, Casa Brugal, and Cochón Calvo & Co., prominent members of the northern Cibao elite (Moya Pons, 1992a:31–33). Again, Elías Gadala María, a native of El Salvador, offered capital investments at a time when the Dominican Republic badly needed the development of a textile industry that could supply national demand (Moya Pons, 1992a:48–57). With Trujillo's protection, he became one of the most important industrialists in the country. Within a three-year period he had bought textile factories, sisal plantations, salt and gypsum mines, a sack- and cord-making factory, and a glass plant. When Gadala Mará came under fire from local businessmen unable to compete with him, Trujillo consistently supported him with special concessions in an effort to diversify the industrial base of the nation. These concessions to foreigners who brought capital to industrialize the country indicated that Trujillo was aware that his elite was unable to industrialize the country using its own resources. The foreigners in question were mostly individual capitalists rather than multinational corporations, and many of them stayed in the country and joined the ranks of the traditional Dominican bourgeoisie.

Trujillo's path to industrial development was clearly aimed at creating an industrial class consisting, in addition to the Trujillist elite, of foreign merchants-turned-industrialists and foreign investors who took up residence in the country and became integrated into the creole social structure. These newcomers, like the pioneers of the sugar industry and the foreign resident-merchants of the latter one-third of the nineteenth century, helped to expand the ranks of the Dominican bourgeoisie. Trujillo's economic development model had, however, some important limitations: it was highly concentrated in the hands of the dictator; markedly dependent on U.S. technology, investments, and advice on production decisions; and extremely vulnerable to sudden changes in the world market prices of raw materials and agricultural products.

The Subordinate Classes Under Trujillo

The economic model that emerged in the mid-nineteenth century inhibited class formation. The sugar industry did not develop an indigenous working class because it tended to import labor from the Lesser Antilles and Haiti; Dominicans were able to live better by tilling their own land. At the same time, tariffs destroyed emerging local industries and prevented the development of an industrial working class in the nonsugar sector of the economy. Industrial and agricultural proletariats were still nascent nationwide. The 1920 census reported that the Dominican population was 894,665 and the population of the largest city only 146,652. The rural population was 745,771 (83.4 percent) and the urban population, 184,894 (16.6 percent). There were 137,764 small landowners, 699 merchants, and 2,274 artisans who owned their shops. Industrial workers and journeymen numbered no more than 19,688, and there were 16,875 domestic servants. Thus, the petit bourgeoisie—traditional small property owners—constituted the largest social class.

The subordinate social classes grew moderately during the 1920s and early 1930s. The Dominican national census conducted in 1935 reported that the nation's population had risen to 1,479,417, with artisans increasing to 23,046, small landowners to 365,185, and industrial workers and journeymen to 22,965. As already noted, the bureaucracy forced an increase in the middle levels of government employment. The number of technical workers and professionals increased from 904 to 5,579 in 1935, and the census reported 10,047 government and private administrators/directors (Gómez, 1979:130). The working class did not, however, experience significant growth. In 1937 there were 31,956 workers employed in the sugar industry, but 21,370 were foreigners, mostly Haitians. Outside the sugar industry, all the industrial establishments of the country combined had only 9,020 workers, employees, and apprentices. The working class would not show any significant growth until after the implementation of import-substitution industrialization in the 1950s.

The 1950s also saw a significant increase of the salaried middle class. The number of technical workers and professionals increased from 12,168 in 1950 to 23,190 in 1960. The lower strata of the middle class, composed of office workers and those in similar jobs, grew from 13,943 in 1950 to 27,360 in 1960. Although these tendencies were quantitatively significant, the petit bourgeoisie was still the largest social class. In 1920 there were 2,274 artisans; in 1935 this figure had grown to 23,046, and by 1950 it had more than tripled to 68,046 (Gómez, 1979:130–132). Undoubtedly this large number of artisans had a great impact on the formation of the working class. In 1963 slightly over 74 percent of workshops had four workers or less, but they contributed less than 4 percent of the sales value in this category. At the same time, 54 percent of the so-called industrial establishments had fewer than 9 workers.

As in the nineteenth and early twentieth centuries, small commerce predominated. In 1935 the commercial census showed that 90 percent of the commercial establishments employed fewer than 5 workers. The 1950 census reported 16,943 merchants, and in 1960 the number had increased to 43,630 (Gómez, 1979:151), suggesting that a merchant petit bourgeoisie was forming outside the mainstream of the economy controlled by Trujillo's elite.

The agrarian situation was strikingly different. Luis Gómez distinguished three groups of agrarian property owners. The first consisted of subsistence units with 12 acres or less of low-quality land without access to the market or modern agricultural equipment; these units could barely sustain a family of five and were constantly in debt. The second group was made up of marginal-surplus units of 12–120 acres, offering the possibility of a modest surplus and relative stability. The third group consisted of abundant-surplus units, with holdings of over 120 acres whose owners produced large surpluses without working on their lands (Gómez, 1979:112). Of the 209,400 agricultural units reported in the 1950 census, 75.6 percent had less than 12 acres, and this 75.6 percent held only 13.7 percent of the total. Owners of abundant-surplus units, who numbered 5,352 or 1.9 percent of total owners, possessed 53.3 percent of the land. Finally, marginal-surplus units included 21.7 percent of the 209,400 units reported and constituted 33 percent of the total agricultural land. Although these figures point to the existence of a significant segment of medium-sized property (an indication of the agrarian petit bourgeoisie's economic strength), they also show that the majority of the peasant population lived in misery, whereas a minority (1.9 percent), the landed dominant elites, enjoyed abundant wealth. This agrarian elite was dispersed in various regions, however, and lacked the political coherence to challenge the dictatorship. It had no choice but to accept political subordination—which made it impossible for it to grow as rapidly as the new economic elite. Although Trujillo's expropriation of the 1930s disturbed the smallholders, the landed elite was little affected.

Trujillo's initiatives led to the development of capitalism on a nationwide scale, yet petty-commodity production continued to be the predominant land tenure system until the end of the dictatorship. Tobacco, coffee, and cacao, the traditional small-scale-unit export products of the Cibao, underwent no significant qualitative or quantitative changes. As in the nineteenth century, Dominican tobacco was of poor quality and was produced on small parcels; 60 percent of the land dedicated to tobacco production was divided into plots of less than 11 acres, and only 3 percent of the tobacco farms were larger than 150 acres. Tobacco producers, in short, faced the same structural impediments they had faced in the nineteenth century. They had no access to loans from the Agricultural Bank, because Trujillo's policy was to support sugar and import-substitution industrialization, not small-scale agriculture, and to let German and Dutch merchants control the tobacco market. Similarly, in coffee production, small-scale units still predominated, and on average, parcels were between 3 and 19 acres in size. Again, as in the nineteenth century, coffee producers had to rely on loans at high interest for financing because they lacked access to loans from the Agricultural Bank (Cassá, 1982b:130–145). Dominican cacao, too, was of relatively poor quality, relied on underdeveloped production techniques, was produced on small, inefficient plots, and depended on usurious credit for the same reason.

Although Trujillo did not support traditional export agriculture, he did achieve great success in turning the country from a rice importer into an exporter. Rice, the main staple in the Dominican diet, received strong state support even though neither Trujillo nor the state produced it. It was produced on relatively small parcels, but in contrast to tobacco, coffee, and cacao it required relatively complex technology and substantial capital investment. In the 1930s production increased some threefold and during the war years there was enough rice both to satisfy national needs and to export. In 1960 the Dominican Republic produced a crop valued at US$19.4 million, outstripping coffee and cacao, which produced US$17.4 and US$12.9 million, respectively. The rapid growth of rice production is only partly explained by subsidies; state investment in irrigation canals for rice cultivation was also crucial. In the 1930s, 20 percent of the land dedicated to rice was irrigated, but by 1950 this figure had risen to 50 percent. Prior to the creation of the Agricultural Bank in 1945, the state acted on behalf of rice producers; once the bank was created, this action became a regular economic policy. State intervention helped rice producers significantly because usury had previously controlled credit (Cassá, 1982b:146–147).

The Trujillo dictatorship's differentiated policy toward commercial agriculture is attributable in part to the fact that the Dominican state had to use hard currency, which was scarce in the 1930s, to import rice and to the decision to promote rice as a form of import-substitution agriculture in the early years of the dictatorship. As for sugar, Trujillo had no alternative but to work with the foreign companies that owned most of the Dominican sugar. Later, he and the state invested significantly in the industry to the point of nearly driving foreigners out of that important economic sector.

Conclusion

The new economic elite that emerged under Trujillo was almost totally dependent on the macroeconomic scheme provided by the state. It would have to undergo a complete political transformation to adjust to the post-Trujillo period. The traditional bourgeoisie, which consisted of merchants and landowners, had no choice but to accept Trujillo's political and economic dominance. For traditional petty-commodity producers for export, land tenure structure and production remained essentially unchanged, and this condition prevented them from exerting important political influence. Because of structural weakness, external factors, such as the Cuban Revolution in 1959 and a change in U.S. foreign policy toward Latin America, led to the downfall of Trujillo in 1961.

Trujillo's success in rolling back foreign domination over the nation's economic affairs can be understood only in the context of international political events. He took power at the start of a world capitalist recession; thus the U.S. was forced to accept a moratorium on Dominican debts so that his regime could survive. He was able to terminate the Convention of 1924 in 1940 not only because the United States needed to enlist Latin American support in World War II but also because favorable market prices for Dominican export crops during the 1940s and the emergence of new international mechanisms of foreign domination, such as the IMF, the World Bank, the Import-Export Bank, and others, allowed him to restructure the country's relationship with the United States. With the capitalist recession in 1958, the Dominican economy began to experience difficulties, and after January 1959, the Cuban Revolution began to effect a change in U.S. policy toward Latin American dictatorships. U.S. political leaders had perceived traditional dictators as instruments for containing communism, but with the victory of the Cuban

Revolution some of these leaders began to realize that the cure could be worse than the disease. By 1959 they were reconsidering their Dominican policy. In the summer of 1960, Trujillo's security agents attempted to assassinate Venezuelan President Rómulo Betancourt. Betancourt had allowed Dominican exiles to conduct a political campaign against the dictatorship in Venezuela, and Trujillo felt his regime was threatened by these activities. Venezuela took its case to the Organization of American States (OAS), which decided to break off diplomatic relations with the Dominican Republic. Under these circumstances the United States decided to look for an alternative to Trujillo. Trujillo of course rejected U.S. suggestions that he leave office and prepared to fight to stay in power. His days were numbered, however, for members of his inner group, with Central Intelligence Agency support, had been plotting to kill him. On 30 May 1961 he was assassinated by a group of men from his inner circle, and the Dominican state entered a new crisis that it could not survive without returning to compromised status.

7

Consolidation of the Modern State, Class Formation, and Capitalist Restructuring

The Dominican Republic experienced substantial social and economic change after the fall of Trujillo's dictatorship. Joaquíín Balaguer emerged as a Bonapartist ruler* out of the crisis of political domination of 1961 to 1965 to effect a modernization that the bourgeoisie was too weak to implement on its own. His regime was, however, unable to overcome the contradictions of capitalist modernization and the decline in the international market prices of Dominican export products. Although the Dominican economy was restructured in the 1980s and the bourgeoisie was strengthened, the Dominican state remained authoritarian rather than democratic.

The Crisis of Political Domination

Trujillo's downfall caught a fragmented bourgeoisie unprepared to take state power. The traditional bourgeoisie had been excluded from national politics for over thirty years, and its economic development had been obstructed. These circumstances had left it with a weak economic base, and the subordinated classes that had emerged over the final two decades of the dictatorship were also inexperienced in politics. Nonetheless, politically active groups associated with the traditional bourgeoisie, the petit bourgeoisie, the middle class, organized labor, and the peasantry sought to organize themselves in the post-

---

*"Bonapartism" is the personalization and concentration of power in the executive of the state. It is associated with the predominance of the executive over the legislative bodies and alludes to the independence of state power from social classes and civil society.

Trujillo period. While the Dominican state was in profound crisis, new political parties, labor unions, student organizations, and free media were emerging, and political demonstrations against the remains of the dictatorship took place almost daily.

At least four political tendencies emerged in the aftermath of Trujillo's assassination. First, the failed attempt to develop an armed resistance against the dictatorship resulted in the emergence of the Movimiento 14 de Junio (June 14 Movement), which took its name from a failed armed expedition against Trujillo that occurred on that date in 1959. Many of the followers of the Movimiento 14 de Junio were also inspired by the Cuban Revolution. Second, the Unión Cívica Nacional (National Civic Union–UCN), consisting of import merchants, industrialists, and landowners was founded to organize all the anti-Trujillo forces. Claiming to be a democratic force, in fact it sought to destroy the Trujillist political apparatus in order to gain direct access to Trujillo's assets. Third, the Partido Revolucionario Dominicano (Dominican Revolutionary Party–PRD), which had been organized in Havana in 1939 and whose leader, the writer and historian Juan Bosch, had lived in exile for over twenty-four years, now proposed a *borrón y cuenta nueva* (starting from scratch) that would include everyone who supported social reforms and democracy. Unlike the UCN, the PRD rejected anti-Trujillism as a formula for acquiring political power. Fourth, a Trujillist group sought to retain power under the leadership of Trujillo's son, Ramfis, who was chief of the armed forces, and Joaquín Balaguer, nominal president at the time of Trujillo's assassination. The United States played a key role in the unfolding of political events. Allegedly concerned with the transition to democratic rule, it changed its policy several times during 1961 in an attempt to respond to the volatile state of Dominican politics.

Trujillo's vast wealth was the prize that inspired constant political struggles among the various emerging political forces. In the midst of the political crisis that followed his death, Balaguer transferred Trujillo's assets to the state. These assets had an estimated value of US$800 million and included factories, commercial houses, service companies, urban real estate, and extensive rural landholdings. Balaguer dissolved the Partido Dominicano, distributing its assets among Trujillist bureaucrats, and in order to lower the prices of consumer goods, he significantly reduced the import taxes that provided government income. His hope was that these economic measures would rally the support of the poor and hold off the aggressive anti-Trujillist movement led by the UCN. The United States initially supported Balaguer in this policy, but when popular support for Balaguer was not forthcoming, it decided to back the UCN in its attempts to remove Balaguer from office. In November 1961 the UCN forced Balaguer to resign and organized a council of state to pave the way for its own accession to power. This strategy was thwarted, however, by the PRD's call for a program of social reforms and democracy. When the first free elections were held in December 1962, Bosch won them by a two-to-one margin, and the UCN had to recognize defeat.

Bosch's political platform was embodied in a new constitution adopted in 1963. This constitution recognized democratic rights for the working class, including the right to strike and participation in the management of companies. It declared the ownership of land in excessive quantity "contrary to the collective interest," and "prohibited private estates regardless of the means used to acquire them." It restricted the right to acquire land to Dominicans—a direct challenge to foreign control in the sugar industry—and prohibited private monopolies and speculation with primary consumer goods (*Gaceta Oficial*, 30 April 1963). Despite the radical nationalistic implications of the constitution, Bosch moved cautiously in dealing with the traditional bourgeoisie. The most radical principles contained in the constitution were never enacted, in part because the Bosch administration lasted only seven months, but also because he filled his cabinet with Trujillists and anti-Trujillists and made sure that the agrarian reform promised by the constitution was postponed.

Despite this moderation, the traditional elites worked actively to ensure that his administration would not succeed. The Asociación de Industria de la República Dominicana (Industrial Association of the Dominican Republic) and the Consejo Nacional de Hombres de Empresas (National Council of Businessmen–CNHE), and others joined the Catholic Church in a campaign to portray Bosch as a communist. Mass demonstrations of peasants were organized by the church to protest supposed communist infiltration in the Bosch administration. Bosch rejected these accusations but refused to limit the activities of the left and progressive organizations. Meanwhile the military and the United States grew increasingly uncomfortable with his tolerance of these organizations and began to prepare the coup d'état that took place on 25 September 1963. Bosch had offered traditional economic elites a modernization program consistent with the Alliance for Progress, a U.S. program that ostensibly supported redistribution of income, agrarian reform, and democracy in Latin America in an effort to prevent more Cuban-style revolutions. The coup d'état, however, put a halt to a populist experiment that had sought to change the pattern of development between state and society. Bosch had hoped for a powerful, interventionist state, whereas traditional elites wanted to restrict state power in order to advance their social and economic interests.

Bosch's regime was replaced by the Triumvirate, a government junta composed of three UCN members. The UCN, however, had no plan for national development that responded to the needs of Dominican society. UCN policies did not address the needs of organized labor and the middle class, nor did they seek to improve the conditions of a peasantry that made up 70 percent of the population. Instead, the Triumvirate's actions benefited the powerful merchants demanding lower import tariffs, the emerging industrialists and local bankers demanding state protection to increase their profits, and the military using their military planes and ships to smuggle in contraband manufactured goods. Organized labor, the middle class, and students saw their interests ignored by the new government and staged massive demonstrations and strikes.

Support for the Triumvirate further eroded as merchants and industrialists saw that the military's contraband business undercut their own economic interests. They also observed that, from exile in Puerto Rico, Bosch had formed an alliance with the Partido Revolucionario Social Cristiano (Revolutionary Social Christian Party–PRSC), a party that promised to restore the Constitution of 1963 without elections. This position received widespread support among labor, professional, and student groupings. In addition to forming political alliances, Bosch directed a conspiracy that eventually overthrew the Triumvirate.

By the end of 1964 the Triumvirate had little popular support but could still claim the backing of the military and the United States. The U.S. embassy, wanting to avoid the unpredictable consequences of another coup d'état, supported Donald Reid Cabral, head of the Triumvirate. This convinced many Dominicans that the United States did not want new elections to take place (Lowenthal, 1977:68–69). Read Cabral was unable to see beyond the immediate interests of his backers. When the military failed to support him, the stage was set for the entrance of the urban subordinate classes (the middle class, the petit bourgeoisie, the working class, and the poor) into Dominican politics.

Those in the military who had supported Read Cabral had been negotiating behind his back with pro-Bosch forces who called themselves Constitutionalists. Courting popular support to buttress their position, the Constitutionalists began to distribute weapons to civilians, and this ignited a five-day revolt (24–28 April 1965) that left thousands dead or wounded and almost destroyed Trujillo's army. Provincial army commanders watched the unfolding events with trepidation as the Constitutionalists, led by Colonel Francisco Caamaño, prepared to attack the San Isidro Air Base, a critical center of anti-Bosch forces commanded by General Elías Wessín y Wessín.

Fearing that the Dominican Republic would become a second Cuba, the United States responded with a rapid military occupation of the country on 28 April. Over forty-two thousand U.S. troops landed in the Dominican Republic, allegedly to save the lives of Americans. The U.S. forces immediately sided with the Trujillist faction of the army, which opposed Bosch's return to power. Santo Domingo was divided into two zones, one controlled by the regular Dominican army supported by the U.S. Marines, and the other held by Constitutionalists backed by hundreds of regular army officers and thousands of civilians grouped into "comandos constitucionalistas" (Franco, 1966; Moreno, 1970). Under pressure from the OAS and after a worldwide outcry against the invasion, the United States created the Inter-American Peace Force, made up of troops from the United States and various Latin American countries, to manage the Dominican crisis until the OAS could resolve the crisis.

From May to September 1965 the Dominican Republic had two governments—one led by Francisco Caamaño, leader of the revolution, and one by Antonio Imbert Barreras, one of Trujillo's killers, who had been installed in power by the United States. The OAS mediated the negotiations between the Constitutionalists and the U.S.-backed government for four months. The Constitutionalists rejected the conditions insisted on by the Imbert Barrera government, which would have disarmed the Caamaño forces and reestablished the status quo ante. They claimed to be the legal government and insisted on restoration of the 1963 constitution. The United States exerted continuous pressure on the Constitutionalist negotiating team, and when an impasse was reached, it attacked the Constitutionalist zone (Franco, 1966: 206–237; Cassá, 1986a:200–215; Gleijeses, 1978:219–255).

In August a solution was finally reached whereby both governments would resign to allow the formation of a transitional government that was to hold elections on 1 June 1966. This transitional government was headed by Héctor García Godoy, a businessman and diplomat. The parties agreed that the Constitutionalist military would be reintegrated into the Dominican armed forces and its leadership allowed to leave the country. In fact, the Dominican police force and the army's secret service made sure that Constitutionalist military and political leaders were either imprisoned or "disappeared," while the U.S.-backed Inter-American Peace Force pretended that it was not involved in Dominican politics. The following year the transitional government called for general elections, and Bosch and Balaguer emerged as the leading candidates. Balaguer and his Partido Reformista (Reformist Party) won the elections. During the preelection period the Dominican security forces had conducted a terrorist campaign against Bosch and the PRD, putting Bosch under house arrest until he left the country for Spain. José Francisco Peña Gómez led the PRD in Bosch's absence and thus emerged as a national political figure.

Although the United States had invaded the Dominican Republic to prevent a popular and democratic revolution that it perceived as a threat to its interests in the Caribbean Basin, the invasion had important consequences for the Dominican state. At the time of the invasion, the state, which had nearly collapsed, was still basically Trujillist in design. The military, the bureaucracy, Congress, and the government ministries had not been restructured during the critical post-Trujillo years. The United States had, however, restructured the Dominican military during the occupation, placing it under direct U.S. command and assuming total responsibility for the payment of salaries, clothing, food, and military equipment. It had also taken control of the nonmilitary apparatus of the state, paid salaries, and placed U.S. agents in important government posts, for example, in the ministries of finance, agriculture, industry and commerce, health, education, and communications, and in the Internal Revenue Services, the Central Bank, the Reserve Bank, the National Office of Statistics, and other decentralized government agencies.

The revolution of 1965 and the subsequent U.S. intervention demonstrated that no one social group, class, or combination of these was powerful enough to rule with even the appearance of legitimacy. Because the United States did not intend to turn the Dominican Republic into a colony, a mediator among the various classes and fractions of classes was called for—and this mediator was Joaquín Balaguer. He did not represent any clearly defined group or social class that was capable of fostering a national political project, but he did offer a record of continuous service to Trujillo and a constituency in Trujillo's army and government bureaucracy. He also inherited the loyalty of the Dominican peasantry, which under Trujillo's hegemony had been a traditional source of recruits for the military. Balaguer became a sort of Bonapartist ruler in the midst of a generalized crisis of hegemony.

Historically, Bonapartist regimes have emerged when the bourgeoisie lacked social and political power. They are characterized by the increasing autonomy of the state in relation to the dominant elites. The powerless traditional elites and the Trujillist elite had no alternative but to depend on a ruler who would exercise power on their behalf and attempt to provide the necessary conditions for the modernization of society (Marx, 1978:127–128; Draper, 1977:398–409; Lozano, 1985:49–66; Cassá, 1986a:260–272). In contrast to classical Bonapartism, in which the ruler emerges from a "catastrophic equilibrium" among the different factions of the bourgeoisie (Gramsci, 1973:219), Balaguer's regime surfaced because of the structural and historical weaknesses of the bourgeoisie that had precipitated the revolution. In these circumstances, however, a foreign military intervention—a "third force"—was necessary to secure the defeat of the Constitutionalist forces that sought to restore Bosch to power.

The Balaguer regime was the product of the U.S. invasion and therefore had to respond to its foreign backers. Balaguer was aware that his duty was to create sufficient political stability for international capital to expand into the Dominican Republic and for various fractions of the business elite to accumulate capital under state protection. Beyond this, he brought the military and civil bureaucracies into his political designs, turning them into economic actors whose interests would eventually come into conflict with those of the traditional elites (Lozano, 1985:65; Cassá, 1986a:271–273). Recognizing the conflicting political and economic forces around him, he tried to convince everyone that he was above class or group interests. In a 1970 speech to the Comisión Nacional de Desarrollo (National Development Commission–

CND), a consulting body to the president composed of business leaders and prominent citizens, he said:

> What is special about this organism [the CND] is that it embodies representatives of all interests: banking, commerce, agriculture, cattle, etc., i.e., the so-called oligarchy, as well as the working class and those organisms dedicated to humanitarian enterprises or purely social activities. The National Government thus has the opportunity to learn what they think about the basic problems related to our development and seriously to balance their points of view. What is important is that the government attend to this open debate as a simple spectator and ... reserve the sovereign right to make a decision at the opportune moment without any kind of coercion or extraneous interference. (Balaguer, 1970)

Both dominated and dominant classes were subordinated to Balaguer as a broker in the political decision-making process. The executive thus developed into an intermediary among the various classes and fractions of classes, and in this sense, Balaguer's persona took the place of political parties. The dominant elites had to entrust their interests to Balaguer, who claimed to represent the "interest of the whole society."

Consolidation of Political Power and Class Formation

When Balaguer took power on 1 July 1966 the first item on his political agenda was to provide "order" and "social peace," in other words, to destroy the popular movement. The Dominican security forces terrorized those who had participated in or sympathized with the revolution, targeting organized labor, student organizations, and leftist political parties as enemies of the state. State-sponsored terrorist groups secretly killed hundreds and jailed thousands during Balaguer's twelve years in office. His campaign of terror crushed the left and deepened a crisis within the PRD, the most important opposition party. Political differences divided the PRD in 1973 as Bosch turned left, having temporarily lost his faith in representative democracy after reading Karl Marx, and Peña Gómez emerged as the leader of the PRD's moderate wing. Bosch founded a new party, the Partido de la Liberación Dominican (Dominican Liberation Party–PLD) with leftist PRD dissenters. Balaguer used the PRD political divisions to his benefit and continued to press his enemies with police terror. Political repression reached such a pitch in the early 1970s that leftists and democratic opposition leaders could not safely walk the streets of Santo Domingo. The PRD withdrew from the 1974 elections, and Balaguer ran practically unopposed.

At the same time that his police were persecuting the left and the democratic opposition in the cities, Balaguer was courting the support of the peasantry by using state resources to build roads, hydroelectric projects, irrigation works, schools, and churches in the countryside. Recognizing that the peasantry made up more than one-half of the population of the country, he used his historical ties to Trujillism to portray himself as a leader of the peasantry, and Dominican peasants voted for Balaguer consistently throughout his years in office. Balaguer traveled in his helicopter to the most remote areas of the country to inaugurate public works and to secure the support of the peasantry (as he continued to do into the 1990s). In the early 1970s he even sponsored an agrarian reform, ostensibly to improve the harsh conditions of rural life, but in fact to modernize capitalist agriculture and foster industrialization.

When Balaguer took office in 1966, part of the institutional infrastructure needed for the growth of the local industrial and financial bourgeoisie was already in place, created by the transitional government that had preceded him in order to reinforce the state. A presidential commission had been set up to support the executive by organizing government programs. A national development commission had been founded to formulate development policies, draw up the national budget, and do long-range planning. A technical ministry had been established to coordinate the various presidential commissions and autonomous government institutions most concerned with economic development, and Balaguer used this ministry to control the different government departments. The transitional government had also established the Corporación de Fomento Industrial (Corporation for Industrial Development) to promote the development of the nonsugar industrial sector. Trujillo's enterprises were organized into a company through the Corporación de Empresas Estatales (State Enterprises Corporation). The Monetary Board was given extraordinary powers to control the Central Bank and achieve currency stabilization. Last but not least, there was legislation to help develop the banking system and to promote the development of the financial bourgeoisie (Cassá, 1986a:223).

The creation of infrastructure by the transitional government was enhanced by extensive U.S. economic and technical assistance. During the first year of the intervention, the United States spent US$122 million. U.S. economic assistance reached US$133 million every year from 1967 to 1969, most of it in the form of donations and long-term loans administered by the Agency for International Development (AID). Although U.S. economic assistance decreased from 1969 to 1973, on the average it still amounted to US$78 million per year (Moya Pons, 1992b:542–544). This assistance was essential to Balaguer's survival of his first term. It gave him a degree of freedom in relation to the traditional Dominican economic elites and made him the key intermediary between the United States, local elites, and the Dominican people.

Aware that his regime depended on how well he served his international backers, Balaguer initiated economic policy that went beyond providing order and social peace to create basic industrial infrastructure, guaranteed wages, and economic incentives to attract foreign capital and to encourage investment by local capitalists. Like Trujillo, Balaguer adopted a policy of import-substitution industrialization that rode the tide of high world market prices for export products such as coffee, tobacco, and cacao. His industrial policy was geared toward forging an industrial class while minimizing the state industrial sector (Balaguer, 1988:296–297). Dominican industrial sectors were still very weak in the 1970s and could grow only as partners of international capital and under state protection.

Legislation protected three categories of industrial activity *Gaceta Oficial,* 23 April 1968). In category A were industries that produced exclusively for export; they were given incentives such as duty-free import of industrial inputs and machinery for ten years and were entirely tax-exempt if their main business was abroad—a great incentive to foreign investors and multinationals. (If their main business was in the Dominican Republic, they received 50–70 percent exemption). Category B consisted of import-substitution industries, and it allowed a 95 percent exemption for the import of industrial inputs and machinery. Even so, Dominican businessmen thought that this category did not offer enough incentives, and few applied for its protection. Category C included existing or new industries that used domestic raw materials or produced for the internal market. Protection under this category depended on profitability, an obviously ambiguous concept that made it possible for most industries to apply for duty-free import of raw materials, machinery, and tax incentives through the reinvestment of profits.

Industrialization under this legislation was excessively dependent on protective tariffs. The state and the international lending agencies provided financing for industrial development programs. From 1966 to 1978 the Fondo de Inversión para el Desarrollo (Investment Fund for Development–FIDE) channeled nearly US$136.3 million to the industrial sectors. Industry received 60 percent (US$81.7 million) of the FIDE's investment funds; land and cattle received only 28 percent (US$39.9 million) (Lozano, 1985:85). In addition to the FIDE, private banks and real estate firms contributed nearly US$277 million in loans to the productive sectors. Again, industry was the main beneficiary, receiving 57.6 percent (US$157.9 million). It is apparent that the FIDE functioned as a state agency for promoting the development of an industrial bourgeoisie. This industrial policy did not, however, favor local over foreign capitalists; although import tariffs were a key element, multinational corporations also received favorable treatment.

Balaguer's model, like Trujillo's, was overdependent on the United States for capital, technology, and industrial inputs. Dominican industries basically became assembly plants; parts were imported nearly duty-free, assembled, and sold in the captive domestic market. Tariff protection, tax exemption, the small size of the Dominican market, and the family-like structure of local capital favored the development of monopolies. Again, as in the 1950s, Dominican industrial development had a monopolistic character. Under Trujillo it had been monopoly controlled by one family; under Balaguer it was diversified control by monopolies formed with particular industries.

Banks played a leading role in this model. Both newly established foreign banks and the emergent Dominican banking industry profited enormously in the administration of foreign loans. The AID lent US$25 million to the Dominican state in 1962, and the United States released US$22.7 million that had been frozen as a result of earlier diplomatic and economic sanctions against Trujillo. Another source of growth for the local banking industry was the measurable increase in savings and fixed-term deposits during the early 1960s. The value of savings accounts tripled, rising from US$12.8 million in 1960 to US$36.5 million in 1965, while state deposits went from US$101.8 million to US$160 million (Lozano, 1985:178–185; Moya Pons, 1989:28–89). Foreign banks still controlled a significant share of Dominican banking, however. They channeled most of the FIDE's investment funds and controlled 46.6 percent of all the private bank loans to industry. Among local banks, the national reserve bank had 20.3 percent ($US10.4 million) and the rest of the local private banks 33.1 percent (US$16.8 million) (Lozano, 1985: 87).

The emergence of a dependent financial and industrial bourgeoisie was the most important development of the Balaguer administration. This new class emerged under state protection but remained subordinated to foreign capital. Domestic capital formation was dramatic. Under Trujillo, direct investment had been restricted, and in 1958 foreign investment accounted for only US$120 million, of which U.S. companies owned over 80 percent, mostly concentrated in mining and sugar. Balaguer's regime offered a favorable environment for foreign investment, and several major corporations invested in the country, including Falconbridge, U.S.-Canadian Consortium, Gulf and Western, CODETEL (a subsidiary of GTE), Nestlé, and Philip Morris. These corporations joined First National City Bank, Chase Manhattan Bank, and Shell, which had had investments in the country prior to 1966. Foreign investment reached almost US$1 billion for the period from 1966 to 1971, most of this from just a few corporations. From 1966 to 1974, five corporations claimed 65.4 percent of all foreign investment, totaling US$401.6 million. A substantial portion of this investment went to mining, sugar, tourism, banking, and commercial services. The impact of this investment on Dominican society was overwhelming. Foreign banks controlled most of the credit granted to industry, and direct foreign investment controlled the leading sectors of the economy. For example, Falconbridge, ALCOA, and Rosario Resources controlled mining, CODETEL controlled telecommunications, and Gulf and Western developed a commercial empire that dominated sugar and its derivatives, a significant portion of private construction, finance, tourism, and manufacturing for export. Gulf and Western received government concessions to operate the first free-trade zone in the Dominican Republic. The industrial and financial bourgeoisie had no alternative but to grow in subordination to foreign capital. Dominicans continued to dominate the traditional export sectors—tobacco, coffee, cacao, land, and cattle—but these sectors had not changed their productive methods significantly even though they had begun to receive credit.

Despite Balaguer's success in attracting foreign capital and modernizing Dominican society, his Bonapartist regime confronted at least two important obstacles that prevented it from staying in power beyond 1978. First, the civilian and military bureaucracies were given free rein to enrich themselves; Balaguer once asserted that corruption stopped at his desk. His supporters profited from infrastructure improvements, receiving government contracts to build roads, public schools, public housing, hydroelectric projects, and irrigation waterways. Through the Dominican Sugar Council, civilians were allowed to speculate in sugar, and the middle and higher ranks of the military received concessions to grow sugar for the government's mills, all inherited from Trujillo. As a result, from 1966 to 1978 military landowners controlled 40 percent of the sugar harvested. These concessions secured the loyalty of military leaders, who became dominant figures in the state's most important economic activity.

When Balaguer began his third term in 1974, civilian and military bureaucrats had grown into an economic group whose interests conflicted with those of the local industrial and financial bourgeoisie. They supported Balaguer only in exchange for access to government largesse; they sought to use state power for their own benefit while the revenues for expanding their economic activities diminished (Lozano, 1985:253–254). Conflict between these bureaucrats and the dependent industrial and financial bourgeoisie emerged when the export sector of the economy entered a crisis. Sugar prices in the U.S. preferential market had risen steadily from 6.9 cents a pound in 1970 to 14.2 cents in 1974 and to 60 cents in the mid-1970s. They had also increased in the international market, moving from 3.7 cents a pound in 1970 to 19.12 cents in 1974 and to 60 cents in 1975 (Lozano, 1985:205). After 1976, however, sugar prices declined sharply, forcing a drop in sugar production. For nearly one hundred years, sugar had been the country's main export product. Trujillo had taken advantage of higher sugar prices to initiate import-substitution industrialization in the 1940s and 1950s. Under Balaguer, the state owned most of the Dominican sugar industry and used the profits to subsidize industrialization, but the drop in international sugar prices after 1976 diminished its ability to do this. Balaguer's Bonapartist regime was no longer indispensable to the bourgeoisie; the bureaucrats were in fact much more dependent on state resources. As Balaguer's position eroded from 1975 to 1978, the bourgeoisie began to look for alternatives.

The political situation of the country changed with the dramatic decline in state revenues. Reduced government income made it more difficult for Balaguer to maintain his large political clientele and to continue social welfare programs. Middle-class organizations, organized labor, and student associations began to reorganize after the crushing defeats of the early 1970s and to hold demonstrations and strikes. Police repression could not stop the rising protests, and by 1978 large segments of the peasantry had joined the opposition led by the PRD. Although the protest was insufficient to bring Balaguer to his knees, it was significant because the classes and fractions of classes that had supported him from 1966 to 1976 were now politically divided.

Meanwhile, the PRD had been preparing itself as an alternative to Balaguer and had gained respectability by moving from a left-leaning populist position to a more moderate one after Bosch resigned in 1970. It joined the Socialist International, a social democratic umbrella organization, in 1976 and obtained that body's political support. At the same time it courted the middle class, significant sectors of organized labor, portions of the peasantry, important factions of the local bourgeoisie, and the Washington liberal establishment, recently reinforced by the election of President Jimmy Carter. The PRD presented itself as a viable political alternative that did not threaten the established economic order and selected Antonio Guzmán, a conservative landowner, as its candidate for the 1978 elections. Despite campaign threats by groups associated with Balaguer's Partido Reformista and the military, the PRD candidate drew considerable support from the population. Tensions increased, however, when the ballot count, which showed Guzmán winning, was halted by the military. With a coup d'état seeming likely, Carter intervened to pressure Balaguer into a compromise solution known as the *fallo histórico* (historical decision). The compromise gave Balaguer four provinces actually won by the PRD, leaving him in control of Congress. In exchange, the PRD received the presidency, with Guzmán taking 51.7 percent of the vote to Balaguer's 42.1 percent. This solution assured Washington that a PRD government would be restricted by Balaguer's control of the legislature, and its interests in the island republic were not threatened (*Ahora!*, 1990; Maríñez, 1982; Espinal, 1992). Although it violated Dominican national sovereignty, Carter's intervention made it possible for the PRD to attain power. Once in power, the PRD initiated a process of democratic opening that eventually allowed for genuinely competitive elections, albeit still under the watchful eye of the United States.

U.S. intervention in Dominican political affairs had once again played an important role in the process of social and political change. The United States, having helped to install Balaguer's Bonapartist regime, contributed to the regime's removal when it proved unable to overcome the contradictions of capitalist modernization and the drop in the international market price for the main Dominican export product. Balaguer seemed not to read the signs of the times, and the bourgeoisie found a political alternative in the PRD.

The State and Capitalist Restructuring

The PRD promised to push forward the social reforms that Balaguer had failed to accomplish. It had widespread popular support and enjoyed the backing of the United States and the Socialist International. Guzmán took advantage of Balaguer's unpopularity and his own U.S. support to remove Balaguer's backers from the upper echelons of the military. He also freed political prisoners and allowed political exiles to return home. These measures gave him a degree of legitimacy in the eyes of many Dominicans and created the conditions for a more open and democratic society. This legitimacy proved short-lived, however, for it became apparent that Guzmán had dismissed the *balagueristas* only to appoint his relatives to their positions. Corruption was rampant, and the PRD began to distance itself from the administration it had brought to power. The PRD leaders, José Francisco Peña Gómez and Salvador Jorge Blanco, became vocal critics of the Guzmán administration.

Guzmán's economic policy was based on the expansion of public spending in order to boost aggregate demand. His advisers believed that if foreign trade contracted it could be replaced by increased private investment, provided the state increased spending in consumption only. This policy led to the growth of government employment from 129,161 in 1978 to 201,301 in 1982. The expected private investment did not materialize, but government spending increased to nearly 85 percent of state revenues. The necessity to borrow to pay public employees was a clear sign that Guzmán's policy was a failure. The business community urged him to implement adjustment policies, including devaluation of the Dominican peso, strict control of public spending, and reduction of the money supply and of current-account and fiscal deficits, but these measures were highly unpopular. Guzmán was trapped, because instead of supporting these adjustment policies the PRD was looking forward to the 1982 elections.

Salvador Jorge Blanco was the winner of those elections, and his administration (1982–1986) represented the second attempt by the PRD to implement reform of the Dominican economy and society. Jorge Blanco had promised to complement political democracy with economic democracy, but his action was constrained by Guzmán's public spending policies and changes in the economy. The public deficit had reached unprecedented levels (an average of 5.9 percent of the gross national product from 1978 to 1983, in contrast to an average of 0.15 percent from 1970 to 1977). The average current-account deficit had tripled over the same period (Ceara Hatton, 1991:9),

while the 1982 trade deficit had increased to US$488 million. This is a signifi-
cant sum if one considers that Dominican exports were worth only US$768
million, whereas imports increased to US$1.2 billion. Jorge Blanco ignored
his campaign promises when in his inaugural speech on 16 August 1982 he
announced IMF–style reforms, including the reduction of public spending.

Jorge Blanco's agreements with the IMF included the introduction of a
sales tax, reduction and strict control of public spending, reduction of the
money supply, greater controls on imports, high interest rates, and a devaluation of the Dominican peso. The results of these adjustment policies were
judged positive by the IMF because they reduced current-account and fiscal
deficits, but they produced economic stagnation and a constant decline in the
standard of living of the population. Annual income per capita declined from
US$1,180 in 1981 to US$790 in 1985. The severity of socioeconomic conditions is best illustrated by the fact that in the late 1980s one-half of the population registered per capita income below the poverty line and 60 percent
lacked access to basic public services (Vaitsos, 1993:1). The middle and working classes saw their standard of living drop as a series of corruption scandals
surfaced. As Guzmán had, Jorge Blanco confronted the opposition of a faction within the PRD, this one headed by Jacobo Majluta, president of the
Senate. Majluta blocked a series of international loans and constitutional reforms, forcing the president to impose fiscal measures administratively. This
second round of failure by the PRD, in which the pressing needs of the Dominican people had been answered with austerity and corruption, opened the
way for Balaguer's return to power (Espinal, 1991).

Balaguer discontinued Jorge Blanco's IMF structural-adjustment programs
and instead promoted an aggressive fiscal program to stimulate the economy.
The construction industry was the centerpiece of this second Balaguer administration (1986–1990). In contrast to the PRD governments, which had borrowed extensively from foreign banks and built very little, Balaguer used local
resources to develop numerous public works and housing projects. However,
in the late 1980s the price of the country's export products again dropped in
the international market, thus curtailing the government's ability to subsidize
Balaguer's clientele. Even so, Balaguer was able to arrange alliances with the
PRD to gain approval of budgets with revenues well below government expectations so that he could use the surplus for public works. Furthermore, he
generated investment capital by issuing money without monetary resources in
the Central Bank, thus causing inflation to rise to an unprecedented 60 percent annual rate by May 1990. The circulating medium jumped from 2 billion
pesos in December 1987 to 4 billion pesos in November 1989 (Pereira,
1989). Opposition political parties and business groups criticized these inflationary policies. Polls taken during 1989 and 1990 identified inflation as the
number-one problem facing the Dominican economy. Nonetheless, Balaguer
proceeded with numerous construction projects, including an extravagant

lighthouse in Santo Domingo to honor Christopher Columbus, an aquarium, and a modern racetrack. At the same time he criticized the IMF and vowed that the country would pay its debts—but international lending agencies would have to wait until the resources were available.

With the economy near collapse, Balaguer was reelected in 1990. The PRD split again, with Majluta forming the Partido Revolucionario Independiente (Independent Revolutionary Party–PRI) in 1989 while Peña Gómez retained the leadership of the PRD. The PRD's internal problems and Balaguer's ill-conceived policies had opened a political space to be exploited by Juan Bosch's PLD, which leaped from holding 1 percent of the vote in the 1978 elections to capturing 10 percent in 1982 and 18 percent in 1986. This spectacular growth and the changes in world politics transformed the PLD from a left-leaning party to a more conventional one whose main objective was to attain power. As the 1990 elections approached, Balaguer formed alliances with small rightist parties, but the PLD's leaders thought that it could win without any political alliances. However, they underestimated the significance of the electorate's having split the vote among three different parties since 1978. Despite widespread allegations of fraud, the PRSC claimed victory for Balaguer. In fact, none of the contending parties had a clear majority. The PRD received 23 percent, to Balaguer's 35 percent, and to the PLD's 34 percent; Majluta's PRI received 8 percent of the votes cast. Bosch and the PLD insisted that Balaguer had stolen the election, pointing to the suspension of the vote count by the ultramodern computer system installed precisely to avoid such irregularities.

The State and Economic Change

The various governments that ruled the Dominican Republic after 1978 all had to deal with the economy's move toward dependence on free-trade zones, tourism, and services. The structural-adjustment policies implemented in the 1980s and early 1990s were similar to those applied elsewhere in Latin America, but in contrast to other nations, the Dominican Republic had to adapt to adjustment programs and profound economic restructuring at the same time.

The Dominican economy had been based on the export of sugar, coffee, tobacco, and cacao for nearly one hundred years. In the 1980s traditional exports dropped to record lows, leading to huge deficits in the balance of trade. In 1978 the Dominican Republic exported US$676 million in goods but imported US$862 million, giving it a negative balance of trade of US$186 million; in 1987 it exported US$711 million and imported US$1.5 billion, for a negative balance of US$789 million. This tendency continued through 1991, when exports declined to US$658 million and imports increased to US$1,729 million, producing a negative balance of over US$1 billion. This deficit increased dramatically in 1992 and reached nearly US$2 billion in 1993. This negative balance of trade made the Dominican economy more vulnerable to sudden changes in the international economy (*Listín Diario*, 18 January 1993).

Two fundamental factors accounted for this change: the currency devaluation that resulted from the negotiations with the IMF in 1983 and the U.S. Caribbean Basin Initiative (CBI). From 1947 until the 1980s, the Dominican peso had been equal in value to the U.S. dollar by law, creating an overvaluation that made the export of services noncompetitive in the world market. Dominican wages, already low in comparison with those of neighboring countries, attracted foreign investment to free-trade zones and tourism. These two sectors had begun to develop in the early 1970s, but again, the high value of the Dominican peso had kept them from being competitive. The CBI was a comprehensive policy geared toward advancing U.S. interests in the Caribbean. The Reagan administration perceived that liberation movements in Central America threatened these interests, and therefore only countries that accepted U.S. Caribbean and Central American policies were eligible for the CBI benefits (Pantojas García, 1985:105–128). In essence, the CBI granted one-way duty-free treatment for exports from the Caribbean Basin countries for a period of twelve years. Ostensibly, the arrangement was meant to promote exports from the Caribbean, but it excluded textiles, apparel, crude oil, and petroleum, which were leading Caribbean exports to the United States. In 1986, in partial recognition of the export potential of the Caribbean garment industry, the Reagan administration announced the creation of a "special-access program" that included quotas for certain apparel imports from CBI-designated countries. This program, however, was applicable only to garments assembled in the region with U.S.-made fabric (Deere et al., 1990:153–186). The special-access program was essential for the development of Dominican free-trade zones, because garments represented over one-half of the exports from these zones.

The CBI and the devaluation of the Dominican peso stimulated the development of free-trade zones. Balaguer's legislation had provided incentives to invest in these zones, but since 1969 only two companies had taken advantage of them. In the 1980s the state expanded its menu of incentives to attract foreign capital, including tax holidays of eight to twenty years, import duty exemptions, and unrestricted profit repatriation (Deere et al., 1990:154). It also offered investors low wages and local costs; in 1986, 65 percent of local costs came from wages and only 4 percent from local raw materials (Dauhajre et al., 1989:50).

In 1970 free-trade zones accounted for US$2.6 million of Dominican exports and employed 504 workers. For the period 1975–1988, exports from these zones increased from US$27.3 million to US$516.9 million; some 283 companies had invested, employing 124,000 workers. Exports jumped to

US$686.2 million in 1989 (Dauhajre et al., 1989:35–38). Most of these exports were garments exported by subsidiaries of U.S. multinational corporations rather than by domestic producers subcontracted to these foreign investors. In 1988, 63 percent of the export-processing firms in the Dominican Republic were owned by U.S. companies and only 10 percent by Dominicans, the remaining 27 percent being mostly owned by Koreans, Chinese, Canadians, and others. These processing plants employed 135,000 workers by 1991, corresponding to 4.4 percent of the economically active population. Over 60 percent of the workers employed in Dominican free-trade zones in 1993 were women and received a minimum hourly wage of 50 cents (Safa, 1993:4–8).

Despite the spectacular growth of export manufacturing and job creation, free-trade zones were not a substitute for development. Although they increased the total value of exports fivefold between 1980 and 1988, from US$117 million to US$517 million, the Dominican economy remained stagnant, with an average growth rate of 1.1 percent per annum (Safa, 1993:10). In addition, the free-trade zones were not structurally linked to the Dominican economy: they offered no strategy for development and paid no taxes. Companies invested in free-trade zones because the Dominican Republic offered low wages, political stability, and special access to the U.S. market. If any of these variables changed, the companies might simply decide to move elsewhere. Many Dominican economists still worry that the North American Free Trade Agreement will attract investment to Mexico and away from the Dominican Republic, but this remains to be seen.

Tourism emerged as an important economic activity in the 1980s. The state had promoted tourism since 1970, when legislation provided 100 percent income-tax exemption and 100 percent duty-free imports as well as exemption from construction taxes, taxes on incorporation, and municipal taxes on licenses. The Department of Tourist Investment and Infrastructure, an agency within the Central Bank whose mission was to promote tourism and offer loans to develop the necessary infrastructure for the tourist industry, was created. It was not, however, until the currency devaluation of 1983 that the industry grew dramatically. The number of hotel rooms available increased from 1,305 to 5,300 from 1970 to 1980. By 1985 there were 8,562 hotel rooms available, a figure that reached 19,043 in 1990 and 22,644 in 1992 (Cruz, 1993). Tourist resorts have developed at various beaches, including Puerto Plata, Ciudad Marina, Samaná, La Romana, Boca Chica, Juan Dolio, and Playa Bavaro. In 1986 the state resumed a construction effort that included opening new highways in the south to promote the development of the tourist industry there. The state-led promotion of tourism succeeded in making the Dominican Republic into a popular spot; in 1970, 89,700 tourists visited the Dominican Republic, and by 1992 this figure had shot up to 1.6 million. Tourism's contribution to the Dominican economy in hard currency jumped from US$368.2 million in 1985 to US$899.5 million in 1990 and to

US$1,046.4 million in 1992 (Cruz, 1993). Tourism became the prime gener-
ator of hard currency, while Dominican exports, except from the free-trade
zones, plummeted.

During the many years that the Dominican economy relied on the export of
sugar, coffee, cacao, and tobacco, the state levied export taxes on these products, thus collecting revenues from the export sectors. By definition, free-
trade zones were tax-exempt. As such they did not make contributions to
state revenues or to the national economy other than through wages and local
expenditures. Tourism generated revenues but was also largely tax-exempt.
The transformation from an export-led economy to a service economy with
manufacturing increasingly located in free-trade zones eroded the ordinary
revenues of the state. This transformation diminished the role of the state in
the economy and weakened its ability to meet the needs of an impoverished
population.

As the Dominican state lost its control of the economy, the bourgeoisie and
international lending agencies gained the upper hand. When Balaguer resisted
the pressures of the international lending agencies in the 1986–1990 period,
he realized that the future of his regime was in danger. After 1990 the United
Nations Development Program (UNDP) and the World Bank became Balaguer's principal economic advisers, and even before he was sworn in on 16
August 1990 he had begun negotiating to introduce a series of economic reforms aimed at adjusting the institutional framework to the changes that had
already transformed the Dominican economy.

The public debate over economic reform started when Balaguer unveiled
an economic solidarity pact that addressed the need for structural adjustments
in the Dominican economy. At first the business sector applauded his efforts
to deal with skyrocketing inflation and economic chaos. He promised workers
a new labor code to improve their condition. When he lowered tariffs in September 1990, the industrial bourgeoisie complained about its need for protection. Although he had enacted tariff laws to protect the local industrial
bourgeoisie in 1968, he now neglected their request. A debate ensued over
whether to speed up the opening of the internal market or do it gradually.
The industrial bourgeoisie favored gradualism, whereas import merchants
wanted to reduce tariffs once and for all. This issue divided the CHNE, which
once had brought together the different factions of the business elite; importers withdrew from the organization to form a new group.

Balaguer took a pragmatic approach on the matter, recognizing that the
changing character of the Dominican economy had diminished the role of the
state. The UNDP's experts told him that if tariffs were lowered while the exchange rate was rising, what was lost in lowering tariff revenue would be regained through higher exchange rates (Ceara Hatton, July 23, 1992). The experts were right: lowering tariffs did produce a surge in imports, thus
increasing the state revenues. Even with lower customs rates, state customs

revenues increased from 2,769,379,053 pesos in 1992 to 4,407,737,419 pesos in 1993 (Tejada, 1992). At the same time, the flood of imports had a devastating effect on previously protected manufacturing industries, notably shoe factories, the land and cattle industries, and refrigeration. Increased state revenues convinced Balaguer that he should not hesitate to go ahead with other economic reforms. Stabilizing the exchange rate at 12.40 pesos per U.S. dollar in the period from 1991 to 1992 also favored the two most dynamic components of the Dominican economy, free-trade zones and tourism. An undervalued Dominican peso depreciated Dominican labor, thus making these sectors competitive in the world market.

Balaguer supported the UNDP experts once again when they recommended an overhaul of public finances. Dominican tributary income had declined throughout the 1980s. In 1979 it was between 17 percent and 18 percent of the gross national product; by the beginning of 1980 it had dropped to 15 percent, and it was down to 12 percent by the end of the decade (Vaitsos, 1993:5). Balaguer scrapped the obsolete tax laws and modernized the tax-collecting system. Under the tax code that became law in May 1992, individuals making 60,000 pesos or less per year paid no taxes. For those who made more, rates ranged from 15 to 30 percent. Corporations were supposed to pay 30 percent on profits for the 1992–1993 period and then 25 percent after 1995. The new code eliminated a series of laws dealing with incentives on industry, tourism, energy, and forestry. Other laws were repealed in part, among them those dealing with the free-trade zones, agriculture, and the land cattle industry, which lost tax incentives on reinvestment. The code increased sales taxes from 6 to 8 percent and enacted a tax on selective consumption ranging from 5 to 80 percent. The results of this reform have not been as spectacular as those of the tariff reduction, but they set in motion a process that is expected to modernize the Dominican tax collection system.

Trujillo paid off the foreign debt and created the Central Bank in 1947, and from then until the late 1980s, the Dominican peso had been legally equal to the U.S. dollar; it was devalued through the 1980s and by 1994 was worth only about 8 percent of that. Tariffs, albeit unconstitutional, were implemented in 1991, and the Monetary Board imposed a banking reform by resolution without approval of Congress. On 24 January, the Board liberalized interest rates, making it possible for the market to set interest rates on loans and other transactions. On 11 December, the legal cash reserve for commercial banks was reduced and the selective cash reserve eliminated. In April 1992, the Board authorized the creation of multiservice banking, and new banking rules were issued. Like the tariffs, the new banking code was being applied before Congress had even debated it.

As promised, revision of the labor code was debated by labor leaders and business. The existing code had been enacted by Trujillo in the 1950s. The new code broadened the rights of unions, created labor courts, and established benefits and protections for night shifts, overtime, and contract termination. It applied in theory throughout the country, even in free-trade zones. Although the code was approved in May 1992, it was not immediately enforced in the free-trade zones and in most of the tourist industry. Labor grievances over the free-trade zones continued because union organization was forbidden there.

The Balaguer-UNDP-World Bank economic reforms produced macroeconomic stability. Inflation was reduced from 104 percent in 1990 to single digits in 1993. The shortages of gasoline, food, and fuel experienced in 1990 to 1992 were overcome, and the Central Bank reported that the Dominican economy showed signs of recovery. The trade deficit was covered by high interest rates (which reached over 30 percent in 1993) and by remittances from Dominicans living in the United States (nearly US$1 billion in 1993). However, interest rates were subject to changes in the international money market, and remittances depended on the growth of the U.S. economy, which was also going through a difficult period of structural adjustment. Further, conservative sources, including the *Listín Diario,* admitted that all sectors of the Dominican economy except for the free-trade zones and tourism were shrinking. The living standard of the Dominican population fell to the level of 1980.

Balaguer's structural adjustment programs and economic reforms cannot be considered positive from either an economic or a political standpoint. The economic reforms were conceived by the international lending agencies and the UNDP. The tariffs and the banking laws were implemented by executive fiat without debate in Congress. Despite the passage of the trade law by Congress in August 1993, Balaguer continued to operate as usual—granting concessions to his political clientele to import goods duty-free. Although the economic reforms were universally judged necessary, critics pointed to the need to combine free-market reforms with education and training for the workers displaced by the failure of Dominican industries faced with foreign competition. They also called for political reforms to reduce the power of the executive, which controlled 35 percent of the national budget, and to give more power to the legislative bodies (Vega, 1993), arguing that for economic reform to succeed the political system would have to be restructured.

Conclusion

The post-Trujillo Dominican state was developmentalist until it engaged in capitalist modernization, encountered plummeting international market prices for Dominican export products, and enacted the structural-adjustment policies of 1980s and 1990s. With the fundamental restructuring of the economy, the state no longer controlled key sectors of the economy and therefore could not impose its policies on the powerful private business sector. Balaguer reintroduced developmentalist policies from 1986 to 1990 without success.

The UNDP, the IMF, and the World Bank forced him to adapt to their economic stabilization programs. The role of the state was limited to providing macroeconomic stability so that investment could proceed without major disruptions. It was expected to continue reducing current-account and fiscal deficits even as the standard of living of the population dropped dramatically. The Dominican state succeeded in providing macroeconomic stability after 1990 by implementing structural-adjustment policies and by reforming the institutional framework that supported the economy. In the short run, however, the success of these reforms was blocked by the persistence of outdated mechanisms of state power.

The findings of this study show that the authoritarian character of the Dominican state is deeply rooted in the historical and structural weaknesses of Dominican society. The regimes of Santana, Heureaux, Trujillo, and Balaguer were the result of a fragmented society whose development has been constrained by constant foreign interventions. Current efforts to implement economic reforms are obstructed by authoritarian legacies in both state and society. Nonetheless, the continuous disempowerment of the state in the economic sphere opens the way for political change and democratization.

8

State and Class Formation in the Dominican Republic: Some Conclusions

Current interpretations of the formation of the modern Dominican state suggest that prior to the U.S. military occupation of 1916–1924 the society was fragmented, heterogeneous, and without a principal economic regulator (Oviedo and Catrain, 1981). Rosario Espinal (1987) argues that the intervention brought political and administrative centralization but not a national state-building project. From a Marxist perspective, Ramonina Brea (1983) also points to the U.S. military government in explaining the origins of the modern state and its involvement in the process of primitive accumulation. In contrast to these interpretations, my historical-sociological perspective has led me to seek the initial stages of the formation of the modern state in the Dominican Republic in the administrations of Ulises Heureaux and Ramón Cáceres.

The study of political power during the early stages of state formation calls for a class analysis. The caudillo paradigm is incapable of capturing the deeper significance of caudillo politics (Cross Beras, 1980; Campillo Pérez, 1966; Martínez, 1985). The approach I have adopted here reveals that class interests are sometimes more important than individual personalities in explaining the development of political power. From this appraisal of nineteenth-century and early twentieth-century Dominican caudillos, it is clear that their political actions often had a hidden class component. Santana and Báez sought to annex the Dominican Republic to a foreign power in order to protect the class interests that they felt were threatened by the emerging commercial bourgeoisie of the Cibao. These caudillos, along with the nationalist Luperón, developed a political alliance with local and foreign resident merchants. Later, Heureaux defeated De Moya's rebellion with the help of a substantial loan from his allies, the Puerto Plata–based merchants. Similarly, Jiménes, Vásquez, Arias, Cáceres, and other leaders developed their bases of support through their ties with merchants and foreign banks.

The rivalries among Dominican caudillos manifested an oblique form of class struggle. Caudillos were either landowner-merchants or men who had attracted followers through their military skills. Behind the clientelistic relationship between caudillos and their followers were economic factors that often outweighed the strictly individual relationship. Although clientelism is undoubtedly significant in relatively undeveloped societies, in the Dominican Republic the political power organized by caudillos was used to promote the interests of an emerging commercial bourgeoisie that had not yet developed sufficiently to produce a ruling elite. The modern Dominican state is not simply a product of the U.S. military occupation of 1916–1924 but is a logical result of socioeconomic and political processes set in motion in the mid-nineteenth century. The interplay between local political struggles and ongoing foreign intrusions in Dominican affairs is a key to understanding the beginning phase of state formation.

The dictatorship of Ulises Heureaux (1886–1899) and the regime of Ramón Cáceres (1906–1911) had profound political implications for the formation of the modern state. Initially, the dictatorship of Heureaux articulated the political and economic interests of an emerging local bourgeoisie based on sugar planting and commerce. This political alliance allowed Heureaux to begin developing a modern state that could provide the necessary conditions for capitalist accumulation. Subsequent monopolization of the sugar industry by U.S. sugar corporations and continued reliance on foreign credit, however, brought about the near-collapse of government institutions.

Heureaux worked to promote the development of the sugar industry and sponsored a series of infrastructural projects that helped to modernize Dominican society. Economic growth under his dictatorship facilitated the centralization of the armed forces, making them responsive to personalized authority. Two railroad lines allowed for the rapid movement of troops, and the newly created Dominican navy facilitated the transportation of soldiers by sea. The telegraph expedited military communication and helped stifle rebellions before a shot had been fired. The state became a self-sufficient political unit and as such began intervening in society to bring about economic growth and the internal climate appropriate to capitalist development.

The political stability and economic prosperity delivered under Heureaux proved fatal to the annexationist cause. The state supported its nationalist writers, and the Puerto Rican philosopher and educator Eugenio María de Hostos received government support to develop a nationalist education system. Although Hostos eventually fled Heureaux's tyranny, his influence, along with that of Pedro Francisco Bonó, Ulises Francisco Espaillat, José Gabriel García, and Salomé Ureña, helped to instill a nationalist ethos in the Dominican people. The state also promoted the idea that Juan Pablo Duarte, Francisco del Rosario Sánchez, and Matias Ramón Mella were the founding fathers of the Dominican nation. The words and music of the Dominican national anthem were written in the 1890s. The Dominican state seemed to be promoting the development of the nation. This early development was hindered, however, by the authoritarianism of the state and the new mode of integration of the Dominican economy into the international capitalist system.

The dictatorship of Heureaux was based on the support of a carefully worked-out alliance with the newly emerging bourgeoisie based on sugar planting and commerce. Heureaux was aware of the economic and political nature of this alliance and sought European and North American credit in order to establish relative political autonomy from the planters and merchants. European credit subordinated the state to foreign bondholders by increasing the external debt to unprecedented levels. Merchants continued to play a role in Dominican finance, but as the North American SDIC took over Dominican customs houses and finances, those merchants were steadily marginalized as government creditors.

The integration of Dominican finances into the international credit system restricted the power of the dictatorship. Under pressure from local political elites and incapable of keeping up subsidies to quiet his opponents, Heureaux was forced to borrow excessively. When he could get no more loans, he issued inflated currency. His long-time associates, the domestic sugar planters and merchants, rejected this measure, and the ensuing crisis brought about his assassination in 1899 and the near-collapse of the state. Despite these failures, Heureaux's dictatorship had begun to give the Dominican state national scope and self-sufficiency.

The regime of Ramón Cáceres was a second attempt to lay the foundation for a modern state in the Dominican Republic. The pioneers of the sugar industry and merchants were excluded from the mainstream of the economy by U.S. sugar corporations and bankers. After 1905 the U.S. government controlled Dominican customs houses and finances, but a faction of the local elite considered it possible to build a strong state under U.S. hegemony. This perception was reinforced by a traditional Latin American view of the state whereby access to government largesse was a normal way of acquiring wealth. The faction that shared this belief sought reform of the constitution in an effort to expand and modernize the political order.

Cáceres's reorganization of the state under U.S. hegemony further weakened the embryonic national bourgeoisie. An overview of his policies points to the consolidation of political power to serve U.S. economic and political interests. He promoted the development of the sugar industry and introduced comprehensive legislation to effect the institution of modern capitalist property relations. He expanded earlier efforts to establish a strong and long-lasting relationship with American bankers and the U.S. government. The

Dominican-American Convention of 1907 turned the Dominican state into a semiprotectorate of the United States and initiated the neocolonial ties that persist into the 1990s.

The U.S. military government did not fall on the Dominican Republic like a bolt out of the blue. Rather, it rode the crest of socioeconomic and political processes that had begun in the mid-nineteenth century. It expanded on Cáceres's efforts to lay the groundwork for the development of the Dominican state. It undertook the tasks of developing a public works program that established a national road network; organizing a constabulary that monopolized power over society; eliminating tariff barriers, thereby strengthening the economic position of foreign resident merchants involved in the import trade but inhibiting the growth of traditional export agriculture; legalizing the false titles held by sugar and timber companies, legitimating the actions of the military government during the occupation; and incorporating the Dominican state into the U.S. sphere of influence. These achievements undoubtedly helped to complete the centralization of political power and thus strengthened the modern state, but they would have been impossible without the co-operation of the traditional elites. Nationalist resistance to U.S. occupation at home and abroad forced President Wilson and his successor, President Harding, to negotiate the withdrawal of the marines from the Dominican Republic. A new civilian government was elected in 1924, and all the actions of the military government were accepted. Neocolonial political institutions were established and U.S. economic interests secured.

The findings of this study support the theory that the peripheral state is the result not only of the internal dialectic of local class struggles but also of the contradictions between this dialectic and metropolitan capitalist expansion. This contradictory process was set in motion during the colonial era and intensified throughout the nineteenth and the twentieth century as the Dominican state began to emerge. Like other emerging nation-states in the Caribbean region, the Dominican Republic was too weak to resist U.S. economic and political expansion. Nonetheless, the efforts of the U.S. military government to organize a modern state succeeded only with the collaboration of a faction of the local elites. These elites, structurally weak and marginalized from the main facets of the economy, proved no match for the military elite that emerged after Rafael L. Trujillo took power. Trujillo's dictatorship (1930–1961), and Joaquín Balaguer's (1966–1978) as well, illustrate how neocolonial relations were carried out in the twentieth century and what their consequences were for the consolidation of the modern state. The effects of this authoritarian legacy still linger in the process of class and state formation in the Dominican Republic.

Trujillo and Balaguer used their political power to lay the necessary foundations for the development of a Dominican bourgeoisie. No economic elite rose to power with Trujillo; rather, he led a movement that used political institutions to direct a process of capital accumulation that provided the economic foundation for a new elite. At the same time, he granted generous concessions to foreigners who provided capital to industrialize the country, and industrialists such as Elías Gadala María, Celso Pérez, Fernando Villeya-San Miguel, and others joined the foreign merchants-turned-industrialists who had taken up residence in the country at the beginning of the twentieth century in expanding the Dominican bourgeoisie.

Like the Trujillo dictatorship, the twelve-year regime of Balaguer was the result of a combination of the structural weakness of the Dominican bourgeoisie and a U.S. military occupation. Balaguer's Bonapartist regime, propped up by the U.S. military occupation of 1965, served as an intermediary between a weak bourgeoisie and a powerful social movement that threatened the established but dependent capitalist order. As Trujillo had, Balaguer adopted a policy of import-substitution industrialization that took advantage of high international market prices for traditional export products and massive U.S. economic aid. This policy benefited international capital and led to the development of a dependent industrial class while diminishing the state industrial sectors. The resources of state enterprises were used to promote private industrial development and an emergent banking industry. The upper echelons of the civilian and military bureaucracy were given free rein to become powerful economic groups. When U.S. economic assistance declined and sugar prices plummeted in 1976, the regime entered into a crisis. By the time this occurred, however, a dependent bourgeoisie had developed, and the Bonapartist regime was no longer necessary to protect the status quo.

During the 1980s the Dominican economy experienced extraordinary structural changes that had a decisive impact on the development of the state. For nearly one hundred years the economy had been based on traditional export products such as sugar, coffee, cacao, and tobacco, and over a ten-year period these products ceased to be the engine of the economy. The economy now came to depend on free-trade zones, tourism, commerce, and banking. Manufacturers in the free-trade zones paid no taxes, and the state did not control the proceeds of the tourist industry. Because it no longer controlled revenues as it once did, the state played a much-reduced role in Dominican life. This role was limited to providing the macroeconomic stability that allowed foreign and local capital accumulation to proceed uninterrupted. The IMF, the World Bank, and the local bourgeoisie expected the state to reduce current-account and fiscal deficits, but this increased the poverty that was already widespread and made it impossible for the state to provide basic social services. It remained to be seen, in the mid-1990s, whether a state restricted to protecting the social and economic power of the local bourgeoisie and international capital would be able to keep the poor at bay.

Bibliography

Documents

Records of the Department of State Relating to the Internal Affairs of the Dominican Republic

Letter dated 19 September 1912 from W. E. Pulliam, General Receiver of Dominican Customs, setting forth deplorable state of affairs in Republic, Roll No. 5, Sub. 678.

Letter dated 13 October 1912 from General McIntyre covering arrival in Santo Domingo and investigation of political conditions, Roll No. 5, Sub. 760.

Letter dated 13 November 1913 from North American Consul in Puerto Plata reporting interview with Arias and giving opinion, Roll No. 7, Sub. 968.

Memorandum dated 31 March 1914 describing revolutionary activity of Desiderio Arias, position of Arias in Dominican politics, Roll No. 8, Sub. 1144.

Letter in Spanish dated 19 October 1915 from President Juan Isidro Jiménes to President Woodrow Wilson, Roll No. 13, Sub. 1776.

Memorandum from William Russell to Frank L. Polk dated 15 November 1915, Department of State, Roll No. 13, Sub. 1776.

Records of the Department of State Relating to the Foreign Relations of the United States

Award of the Commission of Arbitration under the Provisions of the Protocol of January 31, 1903, Between the United States of America and the Dominican Republic, for the Settlement of the Claims of the San Domingo Improvement Company of New York and its Allied Companies. Washington, D.C.: Government Printing Office, December 6, 1905.

Message from the President of the United States, Transmitting a Protocol of an Agreement Between the United States and the Dominican Republic, Providing for the Collection and Disbursement by the United States of the Customs Revenues of the Dominican Republic, Signed on February 7, 1905. Washington, D.C.: Government Printing Office, 1905.

Convention Between the United States of America and the Dominican Republic Providing for the Assistance of the United States in the Collection and Application of the Customs Revenues of the Dominican Republic, the Enabling Act, and Other Correspondence Relative to the Interpretation and Enforcement of the Treaty, Proclaimed July 25, 1907. Washington, D.C.: Government Printing Office, 1910.

Letter from Acting Secretary of State Frank L. Polk to Russell, U.S. Minister in Santo Domingo, September 17, 1915. Washington, D.C.: Government Printing Office, 1924.

Proclamation of Occupation and Military Government, December 5, 1916. Washington, D.C.: Government Printing Office, 1925.

Annual Report of the Military Government of Santo Domingo up to End of Fiscal Year, June 30, 1917. Washington, D.C.: Government Printing Office, 1926.

Quarterly Report of the Military Government of Santo Domingo for the Months of July, August, and September, 1917. Washington, D.C.: Government Printing Office, 1926.

Quarterly Report of the Military Government of Santo Domingo for the Period April 1, 1918, to June 30, 1918, from Governor Harry Knapp to Secretary of the Navy (J. Daniels). Washington, D.C.: Government Printing Office, 1930.

Memorandum from Doctor Henríquez y Carvajal to the Chief of the Division of Latin American Affairs of the Department of State (Stabler), April 19, 1919. Washington, D.C.: Government Printing Office, 1934.

Letter dated August 28, 1919, from the Military Governor of Santo Domingo (Thomas Snowden) to the Secretary of the Navy (J. Daniels). Washington, D.C.: Government Printing Office, 1934.

Letter dated February 10, 1922 from the Secretary of State to the Minister in the Dominican Republic (Russell), Temporarily in the United States. Washington, D.C.: Government Printing Office, 1938.

Other U.S. Sources

Consular Reports: S.D., C3.1, No. 08, Report No. 83, 1 August 1884, from Consul H.C.C. Astwood to Second Assistant Secretary of State William Hunter.

U.S. Congress. Senate. *Report on the Debt of Santo Domingo, Submitted to the President of the United States by Jacob H. Hollander, Special Commissioner.* 59th Congress, Session 1, Executive Document No. 14, 1905.

U.S. Congress. Senate. *Statement of Professor Jacob H. Hollander Before the Committee on Foreign Relations on Wednesday, January 16, in Reference to the Debt of Santo Domingo.* Washington, D.C.: Government Printing Office, 1907.

Dominican Customs Receivership, *Report, 1907–1935.* Washington, D.C.: Government Printing Office, 1908–1936.

Dominican Sources

Listín Diario, 8 March 1900.

Listín Diario, 13 November 1901.

Gaceta Oficial, No. 2207, 8 July 1911. Ley sobre franquicias agrícola. Archivo General de la Nación, Santo Domingo.

Memorandum presented by Francisco Henríquez y Carvajal to the Committee of the Senate of the United States, named to investigate the Military Occupation in Santo Domingo, 1921. Archivo General de la Nación, Santo Domingo.

Memoria de Hacienda Pública for 1924. Archivo General de de la Nación, Santo Domingo.

Gaceta Oficial, No. 8758, 30 April 1963. Constitición de la República Dominicana. Archivo General de la Nación, Santo Domingo.

Gaceta Oficial, No. 9079, 23 April 1968. Ley de proteccón e incentivo industrial. Archivo General de la Nación, Santo Domingo.

Balaguer, Joaquín. 1970. Discurso ante Comisión Nacional de Desarrollo. *Listín Diario,* 17 August.

Primer Censo Nacional de República Dominicana, 1975. Santo Domingo: Editora de la Universidad Autónoma de Santo Domingo.

Ahora! No. 1138, February 1990. Las Elecciones Dominicana de 1978 y el Congreso de Estados Unidos.

Listín Diario, 18 January 1993.

Books

Alburquerque, Alcibiades. 1961. *Títulos de los terrenos comuneros de la República Dominicana.* Ciudad Trujillo: Impresora Dominicana.

Anderson, Perry. 1975. *Lineages of the Absolutist State.* London: New Left Review.

Báez, Franc. 1978. *Azúcar y dependencia en la República Dominicana.* Santo Domingo: Editora de la Universidad Autónoma de Santo Domingo.

_____. 1986. *La formación del sistema agroexportador en el Caribe: República Dominicana y Cuba, 1515–1898.* Santo Domingo: Editora de la Universidad Autónoma de Santo Domingo.

Balaguer, Joaquín. 1988. *Mensajes presidenciales.* Santo Domingo: Editorial Corripio.

Bass, William L. 1902. *Reciprocidad: Exposición presentada al Gobierno de la República Dominicana.* Santo Domingo: Impresora Cuna de America.

Boin, Jacqueline, and José Serrulle Ramia. 1979. *El proceso de desarrollo del capitalismo en la República Dominicana (1844–1930).* Vol. 1. Santo Domingo: Ediciones Gramil.

_____. 1981. *El proceso de desarrollo del capitalismo en la República Dominicana (1875–1930).* Vol. 2. Santo Domingo: Ediciones Gramil.

Bosch, Juan. 1959. *Trujillo: Causas de una tiranía sin ejemplo.* Caracas: Librería Las Novedades.

_____. 1982. *La guerra de restauración.* Santo Domingo: Editora Corripio.

_____. 1984. *Composición social dominicana.* 14th ed. Santo Domingo: Editora Alfa y Omega.

_____. 1986. *Capitalismo tardío en la República Dominicana.* Santo Domingo: Editora Alfa y Omega.

_____. 1988. *Las dictaduras dominicanas.* Santo Domingo: Editora Alfa y Omega.

Brea, Ramonina. 1983. *Ensayo sobre la formación del estado capitalista en la República Dominicana y Haiti.* Santo Domingo: Editora Taller.

Bueno, Arturo. 1961. *Santiago, quién te vio y quién te ve.* Santiago de los Caballeros: Impresora Comercial.

Calder, Bruce. 1984. *The Impact of Intervention: The Dominican Republic During the U.S. Occupation of 1916–1924.* Austin: University of Texas Press.

Callcott, Wilfrid H. 1977. *The Caribbean Policy of the United States, 1890–1920.* New York: Octagon Books.

Campillo Pérez, Julio. 1966. *El grillo y el ruiseñor: Elecciones presidenciales.* Santo Domingo: Editora Alfa y Omega.

Cardoso, Fernando Henrique. 1979. "Overview of the Bureaucratic-Authoritarian Model," in David Collier, ed., *The New Authoritarianism in Latin America.* Princeton: Princeton University Press.

Carmagnani, Marcello. 1984. *Estado y sociedad en América Latina, 1850–1930.* México, D.F.: Editora Grijalbo.

Cassá, Roberto. 1979. *Historia social y económica de la República Dominicana: Introducción a su estudio.* Vol. 1. Santo Domingo: Editora Alfa y Omega.

———. 1981. *Historia social y económica de la República Dominicana: Introducción a su estudio.* Vol. 2. Santo Domingo: Editora Alfa y Omega.

———. 1982a. "Evolución social dominicana desde la restauración hasta fines del siglo XIX," in Tirso Mejia-Ricard, ed., *La sociedad dominicana durante la Segunda República, 1865–1924.* Santo Domingo: Editora de la Universidad Autónoma de Santo Domingo.

———. 1982b. *Capitalismo y dictadura.* Santo Domingo: Editora de la Universidad Autónoma de Santo Domingo.

———. 1986a. *Los doce años: Contrarevolución y reforma.* Vol. 1. Santo Domingo: Editora Alfa y Omega.

———. 1986b. *Actualidad y Perspectivas de la cuestión nacional en la República Dominicana.* Santo Domingo: Editora Alfa y Omega.

Castor, Susy. 1971. *La ocupación norteamericana de Haití y sus consecuencias, 1915–1934.* México, D.F.: Siglo XXI.

———. 1983. *Migración y relaciones internacionales: El caso haitiano-dominicano.* México, D.F.: Universidad Nacional Autónoma de México.

Castro García, Teófilo. 1978. *Intervención yanqui 1916–1924.* Santo Domingo: Editora Taller.

Clausner, Marlin D. 1973. *Rural Santo Domingo, Settled, Unsettled, and Resettled.* Philadelphia: Temple University Press.

Collier, David, ed. 1979. *The New Authoritarianism in Latin America.* Princeton: Princeton University Press.

Cordero Michel, Emilio. 1968. *La Revolución haitiana y Santo Domingo.* Santo Domingo: Editora Nacional.

Cordoba, Arnaldo. 1977. *Orígenes del estado en América Latina.* Centro de Estudios Latinoamericanos, Cuaderno No. 32. Mexico, D.F.: Facultad de Ciencias Políticas y Sociales.

Cotler, Julio. 1978. *Clases, estado y nación en el Perú.* Lima: Instituto de Estudios Peruanos.

Crassweller, Robert D. 1966. *Trujillo, la tragica aventura del poder personal.* Santo Domingo: n.p. Originally published in English as *Trujillo: The Life and Times of a Caribbean Dictator.* New York: Macmillan, 1966. In-text citations come from the Spanish edition.

Dauhajre, Andrés, Jr. et al. 1989. *Impacto de las zonas francas industriales de exportación en la República Dominicana.* Santo Domingo: Fundación Economía y Desarrollo.

De la Rosa, Antonio. 1969. *Las finanzas de Santo Domingo y el control americano.* Santo Domingo: Editora Nacional.

Deere, Carmen et al. 1990. *In the Shadows of the Sun: Caribbean Development Alternatives and U.S. Policy.* Boulder: Westview Press.

Del Castillo, José et al. 1974. *La Gulf & Western en la República Dominicana.* Santo Domingo: Editora Taller.

_____. 1981. "Las inmigraciones y su aporte a la cultura (finales del siglo XIX y principios del XX)," in Bernardo Vega, ed., *Ensayos sobre cultura dominicana.* Santo Domingo: Fundación Cultural Dominicana.

Del Castillo, José, and Walter Cordero. 1982. "La economía dominicana durante el primer cuarto del siglo XX," in Tirso Mejía-Ricard, ed., *La sociedad dominicana durante la Segunda República, 1865–1924.* Santo Domingo: Editora de la Universidad Autónoma de Santo Domingo.

Domínguez, Jaime de Jesús. 1977a. "La Economía dominicana durante la Primera República," in Tirso Mejía-Ricard, ed., *La sociedad dominicana durante la Primera República, 1844–1861.* Santo Domingo: Editora de la Universidad Autónoma de Santo Domingo.

_____. 1977b. *Economía y política en la República Dominicana, 1844–1861.* Santo Domingo: Editora de la Universidad Autónoma de Santo Domingo.

_____. 1986. *La dictadura de Heureaux.* Santo Domingo: Editora Universitaria de la Universidad Autónoma de Santo Domingo.

_____. 1992. "La República Dominicana, 1900–1916." Unpublished manuscript.

Draper, Hal. 1977. *Karl Marx's Theory of Revolution.* Vol. 1. New York: Monthly Review Press.

Ducoudray, Felix S. 1976. *Los "Gavilleros" del este: Una epopeya calumniada.* Santo Domingo: Editora de la Universidad Autónoma de Santo Domingo.

Espinal, Rosario. 1987. *Autoritarismo y democracia en la política dominicana.* San José: Centro Interamericano de Asesoría Electoral.

Evers, T. 1979. *El estado en la periferia capitalista.* México, D.F.: Siglo XXI.

Franck, Harry A. 1920. *Roaming Through the West Indies.* New York: New Ribbon Books.

Franco, Franklyn. 1966. *República Dominicana: Clases, crisis y comandos.* Havana: Casa de las Américas.

_____. 1992. *La era de Trujillo.* Santo Domingo: Fundación Cultural Dominicana.

Galíndez, Jesús de. 1984. *La era de Trujillo.* Santo Domingo: Editora de la Lotería Nacional.

Gil, Federico G. 1975. *Latinoamerica y Estados Unidos: Dominio, cooperación y conflicto.* Madrid: Editora Tecnos.

Gleijeses, Piero. 1978. *The Dominican Crisis: The 1965 Constitutionalist Revolt and American Intervention.* Trans. Lawrence Lipson. Baltimore: Johns Hopkins University Press.

Goldwert, Marvin. 1962. *The Constabulary in the Dominican Republic and Nicaragua: Progeny and Legacy of United States Intervention.* Gainesville: University of Florida Press.

Gómez, Luis. 1979. *Relaciones de producción dominantes en la sociedad dominicana, 1875–1975.* Santo Domingo: Editora Alfa y Omega.

Gramsci, Antonio. 1973. *Selections from the Prison Notebooks.* New York: International Publishers.

Guerra Sánchez, Ramiro. 1964. *La expansión territorial de los Estados Unidos, a expensas de España y de los países hispanoamericanos.* Havana: Editora del Consejo Nacional de Universidades.

Henríquez Ureña, Max. 1919. *Los Estados Unidos y la República Dominicana. La verdad de los hechos comprobada por datos y documentos oficiales.* Havana: El Siglo XX.

Herrera, César. 1955. *De Hartmont a Trujillo: Estudio para la historia de la deuda pública.* Ciudad Trujillo: Impresora Dominicana.

Hirsch, Joachin. 1978. "The state apparatus and social reproduction: Elements of a theory of the bourgeois state," in John Holloway and Sol Picciotto, eds., *State and Capital: A Marxist Debate.* Austin: University of Texas Press.

Hobsbawn, Eric J. 1982. "Gramsci and Marxist Political Theory," in Ann Showstack Sassoon, ed., *Approaches to Gramsci.* London: Writers and Readers Publishing Cooperative Society.

Hoepelman, Antonio, and Juan Senior. 1973. *Documentos históricos, que se refieren a la intervencón armada de los Estados Unidos de Norte-America y la implantación de un gobierno militar americano en la República Dominicana.* Santo Domingo: Colección Pensamiento Dominicano.

Hoetink, Harry. 1982. *The Dominican People: Notes for a Historical Sociology.* Trans. Stephen K. Ault. Baltimore and London: John Hopkins University Press.

Holloway, John, and Sol Picciotto, eds. 1979. *State and Capital: A Marxist Debate.* Austin: University of Texas Press.

Jaime Julia, Julio. 1976. *Antología de Américo Lugo,* Vol. 1. Santo Domingo: Editora Taller.

Jessop, Bob. 1982. *The Capitalist State: Marxist Theories and Methods.* New York: New York University Press.

Jiménes Grullón, Juan Isidro. 1975. *Sociología política dominicana.* Vol. 2, 1898–1924. Santo Domingo: Editora Taller.

———. 1980. *Sociología política dominicana.* Vol. 3, 1924–1942. Santo Domingo: Editora Alga y Omega.

Johnson, Dale, ed.. 1982. *Class and Social Development: A New Theory of the Middle Class.* Beverly Hills: Sage.

———. 1985. *Middle Classes in Dependent Countries.* Beverly Hills: Sage.

Knight, Melvin. 1928. *The Americans in Santo Domingo.* New York: Vanguard Press.

Laclau, Ernesto. 1981. "Teorías marxistas del estado: debates y perspectivas," in Norbert Lechner, ed., *Estado y política en América Latina.* México, D.F.: Siglo XXI.

Lowenthal, Abraham F. 1977. *El desatino americano.* Santo Domingo: Editora de Santo Domingo.

Lozano, Wilfredo. 1976. *La dominación imperialista en la República Dominicana, 1900–1930.* Santo Domingo: Editora de la Universidad Autónoma de Santo Domingo.

———. 1985. *El reformismo dependiente.* Santo Domingo: Editora Taller.

Maguire, John. 1978. *Marx's Theory of Politics.* London: Cambridge University Press.

Maríñez, Pablo. 1993. *Agroindustria, estado y clases sociales en la era de Trujillo (1925–1960)*. Santo Domingo: Fundación Cultural Dominicana.

Martínez, Rufino. 1971. *Diccionario biográfico-histórico dominicano, 1821–1930*. Santo Domingo: Editora de la Universidad Autónoma de Santo Domingo.

———. 1985. *Hombres dominicanos: Deschamps, Heureaux y Luperón, Santana y Báez*. Santo Domingo: Sociedad Dominicana de Bibliófilos.

Marx, Karl. 1965. *Capital*. Vol. 1. Moscow: Progress Publishers.

———. 1978. *El dieciocho brumario de Luis Bonaparte*. Beijing: Ediciones en Lenguas Extranjeras.

Mejía, Luis F. 1976. *De Lilís a Trujillo*. Santo Domingo: Editora de Santo Domingo.

Monclus, Miguel Angel. 1983. *El caudillismo en la República Dominicana*. Santo Domingo: Editora INTEC.

Moore, Jr., Barrington. 1966. *Social Origins of Dictatorship and Democracy: Lord and Peasants in the Making of the Modern World*. New York: Beacon Press.

Moreno, José. 1970. *Barrios in Arms*. Pittsburgh: University of Pittsburgh Press.

Moya Pons, Frank. 1981. *Manual de historia dominicana*. 6th ed. Santiago de los Caballeros: Universidad Católica Madre y Maestra.

———. (ed.) 1986. *El batey: estudio socioeconómico de los bateyes del Consejo Estatal del Azúcar*. Santo Domingo: Fondo para el Avance de las Ciencias Sociales.

———. 1989. *Pioneros de la Banca Dominicana: Una historia institucional del Banco Popular Dominicano y del Grupo Financiero Popular*. Santo Domingo: Editora del Grupo Financiero Popular.

———. 1992a. *Empresarios en conflicto: Política de industrialización y sustitución de importaciones en la República Dominicana*. Santo Domingo: Fondo para el Avance de las Ciencias Sociales Domingo.

———. 1992b. *Manual de historia dominicana (Separata)*. Santo Domingo: Caribbean Publishers.

Munro, Dana G. 1964. *Intervention and Dollar Diplomacy in the Caribbean, 1900–1921*. Princeton: Princeton University Press.

Ornes, German. 1958. *Trujillo: Little Caesar of the Caribbean*. New York: Thomas Nelson.

Ortega Frier, Julio. 1973. *Memorandum relativo a la intervención de Sumner Welles en la República Dominicana*. Santo Domingo: Editora Taller.

Oviedo, José. 1983. *Estado, reestructuración y crisis en R.D., 1965–78*. Santo Domingo: Editora de la Universidad Autónoma de Santo Domingo.

Pierre-Charles, Gerard. 1974. "Génesis de las naciones haitiana y dominicana," in Gerard Pierre-Charles, ed., *Política y sociología en Haití y la República Dominicana*. México, D.F.: Instituto de Investigaciones Sociales.

Poulantzas, Nico. 1978. *State, Power, Socialism*. London: New Left Review.

Quijano, Anibal. 1983. "Imperialism, social classes, and the state in Peru, 1890–1930," in Ronald Chilcote and Dale Johnson, eds., *Theories of Development: Mode of Production or Dependency?* Beverly Hills: Sage.

Rippy, Fred J. 1940. *The Caribbean Danger Zone*. New York: G. P. Putnam.

Rodríguez Demorizi, Emilio. 1960. *Informe de la Comisión de Investigación de los E.U.A. en Santo Domingo en 1871*. Ciudad Trujillo: Editora Montalvo.

_____. 1964. *Papeles de Pedro Francisco Bonó*. Santo Domingo: Editora del Caribe.

_____. 1973. *Samaná, pasado y presente*. Santo Domingo: Editora del Caribe.

_____. 1980. *La Constitución de San Cristobal (1844–1854)*. Santo Domingo: Editora del Caribe.

Rouquié, Alain. 1987. *The Military and the State in Latin America*. Berkeley: University of California Press.

Sánchez, Juan J. 1893. *La Caña en Santo Domingo*. Santo Domingo: Imprenta García Hermanos.

Sánchez Valverde, Antonio. 1971. *Idea del valor de la Isla Española*. Santo Domingo: Editora Taller.

Sang, Mu-Kien A. 1989. *Ulises Heureaux: Biografía de un dictador*. Santo Domingo: Instituto Tecnológico de Santo Domingo.

Schmidt, Hans. 1971. *The United States Occupation of Haiti, 1915–1934*. New Brunswick: Rutgers University Press.

Schoenrich, Otto. 1918. *Santo Domingo: A Country with a Future*. New York: Macmillan.

Tansil, Charles Callan. 1938. *The United States and Santo Domingo: A Chapter in Caribbean History*. Baltimore: Johns Hopkins University Press.

Tilly, Charles, ed. 1975. *The Formation of the Western European States*. Princeton: Princeton University Press.

Torres-Rivas, Edelberto. 1981. "La nación: problemas teóricos e históricos," in Norbert Lechner, ed., *Estado y política en América Latina*. México, D.F.: Siglo XXI.

_____. 1983. *Problemas en la formación del estado Nacional en Centroamerica*. San José: Educa.

Troncoso Sánchez, Pedro. 1964. *Ramón Cáceres*. Santo Domingo: Editora Stella.

Tulchin, Joseph. 1971. *The Aftermath of War*. New York: New York University Press.

Vaitsos, Constantino. 1993. *Una estrategia integral de desarrollo: Documento preparado para el gobierno de la República Dominicana*. Santo Domingo: Secretario Técnico de la Presidencia.

Vega, Bernardo. 1990. *Trujillo y el control financiero norteamericano*. Santo Domingo: Fundación Cultural Dominicana.

_____. 1992. *Trujillo y las fuerzas armadas norteamericanas*. Santo Domingo: Fundación Cultural Dominicana.

Vega y Pagán, Ernesto. 1956. *Historia de las fuerzas armadas*. 2 vols. Ciudad Trujillo: Impresora Dominicana.

_____. 1956. *Military Biography of Generalissimo Rafael Leonidas Trujillo Molina*. Ciudad Trujillo: n.p.

Vilas, Carlos María. 1976. "La política de la dominación en la República Dominicana," in Andrés Corten et al., eds., *Azúcar y política en la República Dominicana*. Santo Domingo: Editora Taller.

Wallerstein, Immanuel. 1974. *The Modern World System*. New York: Academic Press.

Welles, Charles Sumner. 1928. *Naboth's Vineyard: The Dominican Republic, 1844–1924*. 2 vols. New York: Payson and Clark.

Wiarda, Howard J. 1970. *Dictatorship and Development: The Methods of Control in Trujillo's Dominican Republic*. Gainesville: University of Florida Press.

Articles and Papers

Báez, Carlos Julio, and Otto Fernández. 1975. "Estado y partidos en R.D." *Realidad Contemporánea,* Vol. 1, No. 16–17, pp. 73–127.

Baud, Michiel. 1987. "The origins of capitalist agriculture in the Dominican Republic." *Latin American Research Review,* Vol. 21, No. 2., pp. 136–138.

Catrain, Pedro. 1982. "Estado, hegemonía y clases dominantes en R.D. (1966–1978)." *Realidad Contemporánea,* Vol. 2, No. 18–19, pp. 9–33.

Ceara Hatton, Miguel. 1991. "La Economía Dominicana, 1980–1990." Tercera Conferencia de Economistas del Caribe, Santo Domingo, 16–20 July, p. 9.

_____. 1992. Interview with the author, 23 July.

Cruz, Elena María. 1993. "Turismo superó en 1992 crisis le deprimió en 1991." *El Siglo,* 12 January, p. 7B.

Domínguez, Jaime de Jesús. 1988. "Desiderio Arias de 1902–1916." *Política: Teoría y Acción,* No. 100, pp. 21–36.

_____. 1992. Interview with the author, 20 March.

Espinal, Rosario. 1991. "Procesos electorales en la República Dominicana, 1978–1990." *Caribbean Studies,* 24, pp. 3–4.

_____. 1992. "Elecciones y democracia en la República Dominicana," in Rodolfo Cerdas-Cruz, Juan Rial, and Daniel Zavatto, eds., *Elecciones y democracia en América Latina, 1988–1991: Una tarea inconclusa.* San José: IIDH/CAPEL, pp. 175–200.

Grieb, Kenneth J. 1969. "Warren G. Harding and the Dominican Republic: U.S. Withdrawal, 1921–1923." *Journal of Inter-American Studies,* Vol. 11, No. 3, p. 425.

Haigh, Roger M. 1964. "The creation and control of a caudillo." *Hispanic American Historical Review,* Vol. 44, No. 4, pp. 481–490.

Hollander, Jacob H. 1907. "The Convention of 1907 Between the United States and the Dominican Republic." *American Journal of International Law,* Vol. 1, January–April, pp. 291–292.

Laclau, Ernesto. 1975. "The specificity of the political." *Economy and Society,* No. 4, p. 98.

Maríñez, Pablo. 1982. "República Dominicana: Análisis de las Elecciones Presidenciales de Mayo de 1982." *El Caribe Contemporáneo,* No. 6, pp. 27–36.

Ortíz, Helen. 1975a. "Algunas consideraciones sobre el alza del azúcar en la República Dominicana." *Revista de Historia,* No. 1, p. 12.

Oszlak, Oscar. 1981. "The historical formation of the state in Latin America: Some theoretical and methodological guidelines for its study." *Latin American Research Review,* Vol. 16, No. 2, p. 5.

Oviedo, José, and Pedro Catrain. 1981. "La Conformación de lo nacional estatal: Singularidad del caso dominicano." XIV Congreso Latinoamericano de Sociología, San Juan, Puerto Rico, 4–9 October.

Pantojas-García, Emilio. 1985. "The U.S. Caribbean Basin initiative and the Puerto Rican experience: Some parallels and lessons." *Latin American Perspectives,* Vol. 12, Issue 47, No. 4 (fall), pp. 105–128.

Pereira, Emilia. 1989. "Bosch dice circulante supera RD$4 mil millones; pide gobierno detenga las emisiones inorgánicas." *El Siglo,* 6 November, p. 4.

Poulantzas, Nico. 1969. "The problem of the capitalist state." *New Left Review*, No. 58 (November–December), p. 75.

Pulliam, W. E. 1910. "Dominican cacao." *Bulletin*, Pan American Union, pp. 637–638.

Rippy, Fred. 1937. "The initiation of the customs receivership in the Dominican Republic." *Hispanic American Historical Review*, Vol. 17, No. 3, pp. 419–457.

Safa, Helen. 1993. "Export manufacturing, state policy and women workers in the Dominican Republic." Unpublished manuscript.

Tejada, Victor Manuel. 1992. "Ingresos fiscales via aduanas aumentan en 78%." *El Siglo*, 27 October, p. 1D.

Vega, Bernardo. 1993. "Porque no funciona la reforma económica en Santo Domingo." *El Listín Diario*, 22 July, p. 6.

Vilas, Carlos. 1979. "Notas sobre la formación del estado en el Caribe: la República Dominicana." *Estudios Sociales Centroamericanos*, No. 24 (September–December), pp. 117–177.

Wolf, Eric, and Edward Hansen. 1966. "Caudillo politics: a structural analysis." *Comparative Studies in Society and History*, Vol. 4, No. 1 (October), p. 169.

Dissertations

Bray, David Barton. 1983. "Dependency, Class Formation, and the Creation of Caribbean Labor Reserves: Internal and International Migration in the Dominican Republic." Ann Arbor, University of Michigan.

Cross-Beras, Julio. 1980. "Clientelism, Dependency, and Development in the Nineteenth-Century Dominican Republic." Ann Arbor, University of Michigan.

Muto, Paul. 1976. "The Illusory Promise: The Dominican Republic and the Process of Economic Development, 1900–1930." Ann Arbor, University of Michigan.

Ortíz, Helen. 1975b. "The Era of Lílis: Political and Economic Change in the Dominican Republic." Ann Arbor, University of Michigan.

Rodríguez, Julio. 1981. "El precapitalismo dominicano de mediados del siglo XIX y los orígenes del capitalismo en la República Dominicana, 1850–1900." Unpublished Masters dissertation, Universidad Nacional Autónoma de México, México, D.F., Mexico.

About the Book and Author

This book offers an analysis of the formation of the Dominican state and explores the development of state-society relations since the late nineteenth century. Dr. Betances argues that the groundwork for the establishment of a modern state was laid during the regimes of Ulises Heureaux and Ramón Cáceres. The U.S. military government that followed later expanded and strengthened political and administrative centralization. Between 1886 and 1924, these administrations opened the sugar industry to foreign capital investment, integrated Dominican finance into the international credit system, and expanded the role of the military. State expansion, however, was not accompanied by a strengthening of the social and economic base of national elites. Betances suggests that the imbalance between a strong state and a weak civil society provided the structural framework for the emergence in 1930 of the long-lived Trujillo dictatorship.

Examining the links between Trujillo and current caudillo Joaquín Balaguer, the author traces continuities and discontinuities in economic and political development through a study of import substitution programs, the re-emergence of new economic groups, and the use of the military to counter threats to the status quo. Finally, he explores the impact of foreign intervention and socioeconomic change on the process of state and class formation since 1961.

Emelio Betances is associate professor of sociology and Latin American studies at Gettysburg College.

Index

Abbott, John T., 51
Agency for International Development (AID), 120, 122
AID. *See* Agency for International Development
Alliance for Progress, 115
Alvarez, Braulio, 61
Amechuzaurra, Juan, 25
Anderson, Perry, 2
Argentina, 106
Arias, Desiderio, 71, 72, 79, 81, 96, 136
Armenteros, José, 41
Armenteros Seisdedos, Jesús, 106
Artisans, 107, 108
Asociación de Industria de la República Dominicana, 115
Astwood, H.C.C., 46, 67
Authoritarianism, 5, 6, 7, 20, 133
Azua province, 16, 25, 31, 32, 64

Báez, Buenaventura, 16, 17, 19, 20, 72, 135
  and currency, 18
  and foreign creditors, 45
  and military, 45
  opposition to, 45, 58, 60
  and Partido Rojo, 57, 58
  support for, 59
Báez, Carlos Julio, 5
Báez, Franc, 3, 4, 104
Báez, Ramón, 79
Balaguer, Joaquín, 114, 117, 118, 138
  and agriculture, 120
  as Bonapartist, 5, 7, 113, 118, 123, 139

and economy, 120–123, 126, 128, 130–131, 132, 139
  opposition to, 119, 124, 126
  and Partido Reformista, 117, 124
  and peasants, 119–120
  public works projects, 119, 120, 126–127
  regime (1966–1978), 5, 113, 118–124
  regime (1986–1990), 126, 133
  terrorism, 119
  and U.S., 114, 121, 124, 139
Bananas, 32, 38–39
Bancalari, Bartolo, 43
Baní, 16, 38
Banking, 4, 7, 43, 44, 46, 103, 105, 120, 122, 126, 131, 137, 139. *See also* Dominican Republic, banks
Barrios, Justo Rufino, 62
Bartram brothers, 29
Bass, Alejandro, 24
Bass, William, 24, 29
Batlle, Cosme, 41, 43, 49, 61–62
Baud, Michiel, 14
Belgium, 39, 50
Betancourt, Rómulo, 111
Billini, Francisco G., 61, 66
Blaine, James G., 48
Blanco Fambona, Horacio, 89
Blue Party. *See* Partido Azul
Boin, Jacqueline, 3, 39
Bonetti Burgos, José María, 106
Bonó, Pedro Francisco, 57, 136
Bordas Valdez, José, 79, 80
Bosch, Juan, 2–3, 6, 11, 58, 60, 114, 116, 117, 119, 124

Printed in the United States
by Baker & Taylor Publisher Services